CATALOGUE

OF THE

LIBRARY

OF THE

YOUNG MEN'S ASSOCIATION

OF THE

CITY OF MILWAUKEE.

ORGANIZED, DEC., 1847. INCORPORATED, MARCH, 1852.

MILWAUKEE:
DAILY NEWS BOOK AND JOB STEAM PRINTING ESTABLISHMENT.

1861.

CONTENTS.

Officers of the Association

FOR 1861-2.

President,
OREN E. BRITT.

Vice-President,
JAMES MacALISTER.

Secretary,
MENZO HIGBY.

Treasurer,
WM. J. McDONALD.

Trustees,

W. L. DANA, E. E. BOWNS,
F. W. PITKIN, J. G. JENKINS,
S. P. LANGLEY, T. WHITNEY,
W. G. WHIPPLE.

STANDING COMMITTEES.

Library and Reading Room,

J. MacALISTER, S. P. LANGLEY, W. G. WHIPPLE.

Finance,

T. WHITNEY, W. L. DANA, W. J. McDONALD.

Lectures,

F. W. PITKIN, J. G. JENKINS, E. E. BOWNS.

Librarian,
E. C. ARNOLD.

☞ Initiation Fee, $1.00 ; Half-Yearly Dues, $1.00.

ANNUAL REPORT OF THE BOARD OF DIRECTORS

OF THE

Young Men's Association,

MAY, 1861.

Members of the Association :—

The Board of Directors submit to you the following report :

FINANCE.

The Treasurer's Report, herewith submitted, shows the Receipts from all sources to be............	$2,883 61
The Expenditures..............................	2,697 68
Balance..............................	$185 93

RECEIPTS.

Balance in Treasury at date of last Annual Report..	$72 74
Initiation Fees..................................	228 00
Dues..................................	1,601 73
Fines...	50 04
Sale of books, papers and catalogues..................	35 86
Net profits of course of lectures	576 00
Lecture by Bartlett..............................	69 25
Received on insurance from loss by fire.............	250 00
Total..............................	$2,883 62

EXPENDITURES.

Printing and advertising.	$58 29
Expenses of Bartlett's lecture....................	80 46

Room expenses	115 59
Books and binding	860 37
Insurance on property	45 00
Rent	400 00
Gas	116 30
Postage	32 78
Magazines	94 13
Salaries of Librarian and assistant	765 21
Newspapers	129 55
Total	$2,697 68

There are dues uncollected to the amount of about $225. The year has been one of extraordinary financial prosperity. For the first time in the history of the Association, the revenue from ordinary sources (not including lectures) has been more than sufficient to meet the running expenses. If the present public interest in the Association can be maintained, there can be no doubt about its future prosperity. But our present success is a pledge of still greater success to come.

NUMBER OF MEMBERS.

The number of members at the date of the last Annual Report, including 59 life members, was		716
New members added during the year, including two life members		234
		950
Decrease by removal	80	
Decrease by resignation	17	
Decrease by death	7	—104
Present number, including 61 life members		846

During the year the number of ladies' memberships has advanced from nineteen to thirty-one.

CONTRIBUTORS TO LIBRARY.

The Association is indebted to E. D. Holton, J. W. Hoyt, Hon. John F. Potter, Col. J. D. Graham, (U. S. N.,) G. W. Featherstonehaugh, Wm. Daniel, C. Adams, Geo. W. Chapman, S. Chapman, Mrs. Chas. Cain, C. Durkee, G. G. Meade, Col. L. H. D.

Crane, and others; and to the Patent Office and the Department of the Interior for valuable contributions of books, maps, papers, &c.; also to W. H. Sherman for several fine photographs of distinguished lecturers.

In accordance with the provisions of the Statute, granting copies of all State publications to literary institutions which have a library of three hundred volumes, the President of the Association has filed with the Secretary of State a verified application for such publications, and has received and delivered to the Association copies of all those of which the edition was not exhausted. These books, contributed by the State, are valuable, and necessary to the completeness of the library. Copies of all State publications should hereafter be secured for the Association as soon as they are published.

Many reports of kindred and other associations have been received, and are on file.

LIBRARY AND READING ROOM.

The number of volumes in the library at the date of the last Annual Report, was		3,798
Number added during the year by purchase		624
Number added during the year by donations		175
Number added during the year by binding periodicals and pamphlets		34
		4,631
Number of volumes sold	49	
Number of volumes lost and paid for	4—	53
Present number of volumes		4,578

We fear that an actual enumeration of the volumes would make it apparent that a considerable number had been stolen from the shelves. The Library has become so large, and the rooms of the Association so much a place of resort, that a proper care for the safety of the books requires that they should be so enclosed that no one could take them from the shelves, except the Librarian and his assistant.

In the Reading Room additions have been made, during the year, to the number of newspapers and magazines. The room is almost constantly thronged with readers.

CATALOGUES.

At the commencement of the year the Board of Directors discussed the subject of printing a new catalogue of the entire Library The result of this discussion was the conclusion that, as a supplement had been printed the year before, a new catalogue was not *absolutely necessary*. They therefore decided to postpone this expense and devote all the funds, beyond what were required to meet the running expenses of the Association, to the purchase of books. Now, however, a sufficient number of books having been added to the Library to form a new supplement, and the first supplement being out of print, the new catalogue seems to have become a positive necessity.

LECTURES.

The Lecture Committee make the following report of the receipts and expenses of the course of lectures, including Gough's extra lecture, and Miss Stevens' reading :

Receipts from sale of season tickets....		$746 00
Recipts from sale of evening tickets...............		708 56
		$1,454 56
Paid to lecturers...............	$532 25	
Expense of printing, advertising, telegraphing, &c.............	163 87	
Discount on uncurrent money	2 44	
Hall rent	180 00—	$878 56
Net profits........		$576 00

The net profits of last year's course, which was regarded as eminently successful, were $463 19.

For the first time in many years our course of lectures has beed carried through without the failure of a single lecturer, whose name was announced at its commencement. Only those who have themselves served on a lecture committee can appreciate the difficulties in the way of such a result, or know what care and energy were neccessary to accomplish it.

On behalf of the Board of Trustees.

CHARLES CAVERNO,

President.

SKETCH

OF THE

History of the Association.

This record is compiled from information gathered from official sources, and from past officers of the Association, and is presented here as a collection of facts, which will have an increasing interest for members, both old and new.*

On Wednesday evening *December 8th*, 1847, a number of citizens of the, then, new city of Milwaukee, met in the parlor of the United States Hotel (corner of East Water and Huron streets, burned in 1854,) in pursuance of a call published in the newspapers, to take preliminary steps for the formation of a Young Men's Literary Association. S. Osgood Putnam, (now of California) was president of the meeting, and E. P. Allis, secretary. After considerable consultation and discussion, on motion of H. W. Tenney, resolutions were adopted in favor of the establishment of a Library in connection with a Reading Room and Debating Society, and for the appointment of a committee to draft a Constitution for the organization of a Young Men's Association. The committee consisted of Messrs. Putnam, Mason, Vliet, Tenney, Holton and VanDyke.

On the 13*th of December* the committee submitted the draft of a Constitution which was considerably discussed and finally adop-

* The Committee are under great obligations to J. R. Brigham, Esq., for valuable assistance rendered by him in the preparation of this Sketch. His personal recollections of the early history of the Association have enabled us to give a much fuller and more interesting account of that period than could possibly have been derived from the bare records of the Association. H. W. Tenney, now of Madison, has also furnished many interesting reminiscences.

ted by the meeting, but at an adjourned meeting, *Dec. 18th*, the subject was again discussed, and the record shows that objections were made to 13 of the 19 articles which composed the Constitution, and the whole matter was referred to a new committee, who, on the *20th of December*, reported a revised document, which, in turn, was discussed and rejected, and the original report, somewhat amended, was finally adopted, and the *Young Men's Association* had a beginning.

The original Constitution divided members into two classes, by age; those over 35 years being classed as honorary members, and required to pay $5,00 initiation, and those between 18 and 35, being regular members, and paying an initiation fee of $2,00. Both classes paid $2.00 yearly. Life members were admitted to either class on payment of $25.00, in one sum, and paid no yearly dues. Besides these classes of members, persons under 18 years of age had the privilege of the library on payment of dues, but had no vote, and were ineligible to office. The offices were divided between the two classes of members. The honorary members taking five trustees, and the regular members two trustees, the president, two vice presidents, the treasurer and the corresponding and recording secretaries. This classification of officers was not adopted until after considerable discussion, and at the end of a year the sytem was revised, the classification dispensed with and the board of officers established, as it still remains. The first election of officers, to hold till the regular election in January, was had in the Common Council Rooms, on the *20th of December*, 1847, though the election was not completed until the following week. A list of the officers is given elsewhere. The Constitution fixed the Wednesday following the second Tuesday in January, as the day of the annual election, and accordingly the first annual election was held January 19, 1848.

So far the proceedings of the Association had shown a special aptitude for debate and animated discussion, but after several weeks spent in the settlement of fundamental principles and the preliminaries for a permanent organization, and after the election of a full board of officers, it still remained to secure members and money to give the Association practical existence, and there were found earnest and active men, who undertook this somewhat thankless task, and to their labor we owe it, that we now have an Association and a Library. On the *5th of February* they reported a subscription of $1513, and a membership consisting of 52 life members, 20 honorary members and 49 regular members. A room was leased in what was then the second, now third, floor of the building still standing at the north west corner of Wisconsin and Main streets, at a rent of $100 per year, "furnished with tables, chairs, bookcases, and other necessary fixtures for the use of the Association," in a style, of which an idea may be had, from the fact that the bills for the same amounted to considerably less than $50. The sum of $500 was appropriated for the purchase of books, and this, together with some donations, and some books received in payment of subscriptions, produced a library, which, at the end of the first year of the Association, numbered 810 volumes, and together with eleven of the leading English and American Quarterlies and Monthlies, constituted the attractions of the Room, which was open on Wednesday afternoon and Saturday evening of each week, under the charge of Edward Hopkins, who volunteered to do duty as the first librarian, and to whose care snd systematic labor during the first two years of the existence of the Association, very much is due.

At the annual meeting in *January*, 1849, the Constitution was revised and amended, as has been stated. The initiation fee was reduced to $1.00 for all members. The time of the annual election was changed to December. During this year, the interest in the library continued and grew, and for a part of the time the Room was kept open every evening. The number of members rose to 146. The receipts of the year were $303.44, which, with a surplus from the previous year, gave a fund of which $219.35 were expended for books, and $119,28 for incidental expenses. Two hundred and ninety nine new volumes were added to the library, and the list of periodicals was enlarged. We may presume that the directors found some difficulty in collecting dues and subscriptions, from the fact that it was officially recommended at the annual meeting, that measures be taken to procure the legal incorporation of the Association in order that it might enforce its collections, though we are not aware that to this day the legal business of the Association has been a profit to any attorney.

The third annual meeting was held *December* 4, 1849, and showed that the interest in the Association was well maintained. The attendance was large and spirited, and the discussion of various matters and plans for the benefit of the Association, continued until a late hour. A committee was appointed to canvass the city for new members and subscriptions; the necessity of a new and more attractive room was urged; a course of lectures was proposed, and other suggestions made and considered, all very much the same in kind, we may venture to say, that have been proposed, considered and discussed, among its members and directors, every year, from that to this. At this time so much interest was manifested that an adjourned meeting was held and more discussion was had, and among other things, it was strongly urged that the only way to reach the object desired, the establishment of a good public library, was to create a joint stock company, whose affairs should be managed as any other business operation. It was however, not found practicable to get the consent of all the subscribers to this arrangement, and that objection to the plan has grown stronger every year since. During this year a lecture before the Association was given by Chancellor Lathrop. A new room was obtained in the then new Martin's Block. Mr. Hopkins gave up the charge of the library, and Thomas Hyslop was appointed librarian and received a small salary. Eighty new members were added during the year, and the course of the Association showed no step backward.

Dec. 4, 1850—The fourth annual election and the beginning of the fourth year of the Association. During this year was commenced the first course of lectures before the Association, and although the lecturers were home men, and the admittance fee quite small ($1.00 for a family, to the course, and ten cents a single admission,) the result was satisfactory, and some of the lectures attracted considerable attention, and gave rise to some newspaper discussion. Debates were also started during this year, in the fall of 1851, and for some time created a good deal of interest and weekly excitement. $360.07 were expended in books and periodicals this year, and one hundred new books were added to the library which then numbered 1320 volumes. The other expenditures of the year amounted to $157.92.

The fifth annual election, *December* 3d, 1851, was a scene of great excitement; not so much from the number of votes, as from the kind, as the record shows the whole number cast to have been 68. But the report of the inspectors, and the tradition of the times, tell us that in the anxiety of contending aspirants for official honor some forgot an article in the Constitution which prescribed the qualifications of voters, and a rigid inquiry on the part of three grave inspectors of election disclosed the fact that some illegal votes had been cast. A long report was made, upon which a stormy debate arose, and even acrimony is said to have been exhibited; but the difficulty was finally surmounted by the remarkable (though the event would show, not unwise,) proposition by the new President elect, that all the officers who claimed to have been elected should resign and allow a new election, which was agreed to. The election was held December 9th, and the result was that some of the self-sacrificing men who had resigned, to save the Society, were again elected, but others were not. It is a matter of dispute to this day, among the most active participants in that wrangle, which party was really in earnest and which only feigned an excitement, to keep up an interest in the meetings of the Association.

In November of this year, new rooms for the Association were obtained on the first floor of the large new block of W. P. Young, corner of Wisconsin and Main streets; but the library had hardly been established there before the whole block was burned to the ground, and the Association was indebted to its active members and friends for saving its property. The small loss sustained was fully covered by an insurance; and the Association next found a landlord in S. L. Rood, and occupied his rooms over store No. 204 East Water street, the entrance at that time being from Wisconsin street.

In *March*, 1852, the Association was incorporated by act of the Legislature, its then Board of Directors being made corporators. The time of the annual meeting and election was changed to October. During this year a new catalogue was published — the second.

October 5th, 1852, the sixth annual election. In the winter of this year a second course of lectures, by home lecturers, was given. They were fairly attended, though they did not draw large audiences, except the two lectures on the "Spanish Inquisition," by the (then) Rev. Dr. Ives. These attracted full houses and made considerable sensation. More profit was realized out of a musical entertainment, undertaken by the Directors, for the benefit of the library. By aid of some members of the Musical Society, and some generously given assistance of ladies and gentlemen not accustomed to public exhibitions of their talent, the concert was well attended and well received, and a net profit of $70 was realized, which was applied to the purchase of books, and produced a valuable addition to the library.

October 5th, 1853, commenced the seventh, and as it proved, a most important year of the Association. At this time, notwithstanding its library and reading room afforded pleasure and profit to its members, they were few, and the Association was hardly known to the public generally — it filled no important place in the public mind. Its reading room was most of the time without visitors. Its annual meetings, which at first had been attended and participated in by many of our best and most influential citizens, were no longer interesting, and passed almost without notice. Anxious Directors all agreed that something must be done to make the library more attractive, and to induce new members to join. Among other plans, it was sometimes proposed to unite with the Musical Society in the purchase, or lease, of some central lot and the erection of a fine hall; but this it was thought best, after deliberation, to abandon, or at least postpone till it was well settled that the Association could pay the rent of its present rooms. About this time a destructive fire left our landlord, Mr. Rood, without a place of business, and he gave his attention to his tenant — the Association. He became Librarian, and by dint of much industry and great skill in making it uncomfortable for any body he applied to who did not join, and very comfortable and pleasant for all who did, he gained many new members to the Association. He went into the street with a subscription paper—an undertaking, at that time, quite too desperate for any body else — and soon realized a sum which put the library and reading room in good condition. A new carpet, new gas fixtures, a change of the clumsy book-cases which had come down from the beginning, for a neat and commodious shelving, and a general brushing up and improvement of all the interior arrangements of the Association, were his satisfactory vouchers to subscribers. The library was kept open during business hours, day and evening, and became a pleasant and frequented place of resort. The great event of the year, however, was the course of lectures. It had at that time become the fashion in other Western cities to call wise men from the East and give the citizens of the new country a chance to see *who is who*, and learn *what is what* in the old, by hebdomadal lectures. It was determined that the Young Men's Association should do this for Milwaukee. It should be remembered that at this time Milwaukee was a far and almost unknown country to lecturers. No railroad then connected us with the East; and in the winter season we had been accustomed to regard ourselves as more completely shut out from communication with the seaboard, than those who only know Milwaukee as it now is can well imagine. But we had a telegraph and a part of the Milwaukee & Mississippi Railroad, and it was decided to try. It happened that the management of the matter fell into the hands of one who had enthusiasm, perseverance and business capacity, and to him chiefly (though aided by others) is due the final complete and surprising success of our first course of lectures by men from abroad, — we so style it, though perhaps no lecture gave more satisfaction than that by our own Mr. Ryan. We need not say, for any one who was in Milwaukee during that winter, that we refer to B. W. Griswold, (now of New York city) who, as chairman of the Lecture Committee, was untiring in his attention from first to last. As a precaution, thought to be necessary, in the first place, a guaranty subscription was obtained from some forty persons to protect the Association in case of loss by the venture. Season tickets, for families and individuals, were hawked about the streets by the committee and other members of the Board, until $700 were realized before the lectures commenced. Advertising was done in all the usual modes, and also by members of the Board personally, who, one and all, talked lectures everywhere, until it was almost true that the chairman and his committee neither did, talked, nor thought anything but lectures continually. The result was a success which gave the Association a net profit of $833.39 for its library and a recognized position as an institution in Milwaukee. The annual report of the doings of the year shows: total receipts, $1,288.54; total expenditures, $1,148.36, (this statement includes only net profits of lectures as receipts); an addition to the library of 351 volumes by purchase; 102 new members added to the Association; a new catalogue, and a prosperous condition of things generally.

October 4, 1854, the eighth regular election. By a change in the Rules, the Board elected at this time continued in office only till May. They were expected to provide a course of lectures, which had come to be a recognized demand of the people, and duty of the Association. Ten lectures were given at a cost of $897.30, and with a net profit to the Association of $358.46. During the term, forty-one new members were added. The expenses, beside lectures, were $596.51.

The time of the election having been changed, to give time to prepare for the annual courses of lectures, the ninth annual election was held *May* 2, 1855. This year our Association formally joined with that of Chicago in obtaining a course of lectures, both Associations being able to offer inducements and to secure lecturers which neither alone could have done. The expenses of the course were $1,606.85, and the net profits were $360. This result was not regarded as satisfactory by the committee, who report that the same course in Chicago cleared over $1,500. During the year 140 new members were added, and 120 volumes were purchased for the library. The total receipts (including lectures) were $2,377.23; the expenses (beside lectures) were about $600.

May 7, 1856—Election. This year it was not thought best to undertake a full course of lectures, to occur weekly, for which tickets should be sold in advance, as heretofore; but the committee determined to secure such as they could obtain of those lecturers coming West, who would, in the opinion of the committee, draw good houses in Milwaukee. Eight lectures were given (among them, three by John B. Gough,) at a cost of $768.32, and with a clear profit of $359.35. About 400 new books were added to the library by purchase, beside many valuable works by donation; forty new members were added. During this year, the Directors concluded (not without hesitation) that the Association needed, and would support, new and larger rooms and a larger yearly expenditure, and the *suite* of rooms now occupied were rented for a term of years. During this year, also, the newspaper reading-room was established and furnished with twenty-five of the leading dailies of this country and Canada. The gross receipts this year were $2,380.19, and the expenditures were $2,303.12.

May 6, 1857—The eleventh year of the Association. At the beginning of this year the Association took possession of its new rooms and materially increased its annual expenses; and the Board found that it required some labor and care to provide for all the demands on the treasury. A careful examination disclosed that, while the apparent membership was much larger, the Association had, in fact, but about 800 reliable paying members, beside 40 life members. Lectures, as a source of revenue, were not available; their novelty had worn off. Indeed, a glance at the names of those who had already been presented to Milwaukee audiences, will show that the Association had pretty well gleaned the field of celebrities in that line, and that there were not many more whom people would pay to look at. Geo. W. Curtis, Horace Mann, Bayard Taylor, Horace Greeley, Ralph Waldo Emerson, Parke Godwin, James Russell Lowell, John G. Saxe, Josiah Quincy, jr., John Pierpont, John B. Gough, Wendell Phillips, T. Starr King, Henry Ward Beecher, George Sumner, and Dr. H. W. Bellows, were in the lists of those who had been here. The Association could not afford to risk a course of lectures, the profit of which to the treasury would be doubtful. For the purpose of testing the question, one popular lecturer was brought here and every reasonable effort was made to get him an audience; but the result was a failure and a loss to the Association, and no more were attempted. The great commercial crisis had so darkened all prospects, that it was often a matter of serious consideration with the Directors how they were to pay the debts and expenses incurred during the year and leave the treasury sound at the close. It was determined to make a special effort for more life members, and at the personal solicitation of Directors, seventeen gentlemen joined the Association as life members and paid into its treasury $425. 142 yearly members were added, and at the close of the year the Board were able to report all debts paid and a balance on hand. The total receipts of the year (no lectures) were $1,351.29, and the expenditures $1,284.35.

May 5th, 1858, began another year of the Association. It will be seen by the list of officers, that at the election this year, the Board of Directors was almost wholly changed. It is but just to those gentlemen who composed the previous Board, some of whom had been connected with its management and had worked for the Association from its start, and most of whom had been associated in its direction for more than half a decade, to say that they did not leave their work, nor abandon their charge, till they saw the Association established, its position assured, and its prospects of power and usefulness bright. They now felt that they might claim a discharge and leave the work to those who might bring to it a fresher zeal, but could not feel a deeper interest in the prosperity of our Association.

The election this year was remarkable for the interest shown and the number of votes cast, being nearly two hundred—nearly three times the number of late years. The Board thus elected carried on the work vigorously. They added to the number of periodicals and newspapers of the reading-room ; they increased the salary of the Librarian to compensate him for increase of duty with the increase of members ; they adopted the plan of purchasing new and popular books as soon as published, and advertising them as they were received ; they made special efforts for increasing the membership, and 296 new members were added during the year ; they added to the library, by purchase, donation and binding of pamphlets, seven hundred and ninety-three volumes. The total receipts of the year were $2,522.29 ; the expenditures were $2,506.17. Included in the receipts was the sum of $786.67, received on insurance to cover loss by a fire in the building, which had nearly been more serious. Lectures were tried again at a cost of $866.10, and a profit of $241.15. The Board also revised and amended the General Rules and Regulations, adapting them to the wants of the Association in its present condition. These Rules were adopted at the annual meeting.

May 5th 1859—This year was a most successful one for the Association. A good deal of interest had been taken in the election, and although three tickets were in the field, the "Regular Ticket" (so called) was elected throughout. Nearly 300 votes were cast, a number of new members added, and a general awakening in regard to the interests of the Association was the result. A new set of "Rules and Regulations of the Board of Directors" was adopted, to accompany the revised Rules and Regulations of the Society, adopted at the last annual meeting, and the Rules of the Library and Reading Room were also revised by the committee in charge of that department. Everything in the power of the Board was done to improve the condition of the Association and to enlarge its means of usefulness. An address to the public was prepared by a committee, and extensively circulated, and a canvass of the city similar to that of last year resulted in a considerable increase of membership. The whole number of members added during the year was 237. A musical and literary entertainment undertaken for the benefit of the library, proved, however, that the public could not yet be relied upon with certainty to support the directors in their endeavors to push forward the institution, as the net profits of the evening amounted to the enormous sum of $4.25! During the year, application was made by the "Builders and Architects Association" for the purpose of forming a union with the Association, and a committee was appointed to confer with that body; but after a full hearing of their purposes and demands, it was found to be inexpedient to meet their wishes, and the matter was accordingly dropped.

The course of lectures given this year proved highly successful, the receipts amounting to $1134.28, and the net profits to $463,-19. The improvements in the library were also extensive, over 400 volumes having been added, of which 155 were donations. Among the most extensive donors, it seems proper to mention Mr. John Hepburn, who contributed many valuable works, more especially in a department of literature in which the library was greatly deficient, and the "friends of the new church in Milwaukee;" who enriched our shelves with a splendid edition of the complete wooks of Emanuel Swedenburg. The Association is also under a deep debt of gratitude to the Hon. John F. Potter, for the handsome manner in which he supplied the library with the public documents at his disposal; and the election of that gentleman as a life member of the Association, was a fitting acknowledgement of the interest uniformly manifested by him in its wellfare. A second supplementary catalogue was published during the year. The entire receipts of the Association for the year were $2153.21, and the expenditures $2080.47.

May 7th, 1860—The election of officers for this year was more severely contested, and excited a larger degree of public interest, than ever before in the history of the Association. The week which intervened between the annual meeting and the day of election (a change resulting from the Revised Rules and Regulations adopted the year before,) gave time for the holding of meetings and the discussion of the merits of the various candidates nominated. By the established custom of the Association the ticket first nominated claims to be the "Regular Ticket," and whatever comes after that is compelled to assume some other name. On this occasion half a dozen different tickets were put in circulation, but before election day, a consolidation was effected, and the field was left clear for the two tickets named respectively the "Regular" and "Opposition." And bravely was the battle fought. Many of our leading professional and business men entered the contest as if the most momentous consequences were depending upon it. Every member was canvassed and arguments the most convincing used on both sides. Newspaper squibs appeared preferring the most serious charges againt the candidates, flaming placards were posted on every available corner, and the rooms presented a scene of excitement never surpassed at the polls on any political election in the city. The result was the election of the entire "Regular Ticket." Nearly 500 votes were cast. It is much to be desired that something of the kind could be stirred up every year, as it undoubtedly tends to awaken a lively interest in the Association, and sets its objects before the public mind in the most advantageous light.

The year proved one of extraordinary financial prosperity for the Association, and to quote the language of the Annual Report of the Directors, "for the first time in the history of the Association the revenues from ordinary sources (not including lectures) were more than sufficient to meet the running expenses." The total receipts for the year were $2883.61, and the expenditures $2697.68. In the month of September a fire took place in the library, but it was fortunately discovered and extinguished before much damage was done. The amount ($250,) received from the Insurance Company, amply covered the injury sustained. During the year, 234 new members were added, making the whole membership 845, a number which will compare favorably with that of similar institutions in many larger and much older cities. One fact worth noting is that the ladies' membership increased during this year from 19 to 31. The course of lectures managed by O. E. Britt, Esq., was one of the most successful ever given by the Association—the net profits footing up to $576. The improved condition of the Association having greatly increased the business devolving upon the Librarian, an Assistant was accordingly appointed at a salary of $4.00 per month, which was afterward raised to $8.00. During the year 624 volumes were added to the library at a cost of about $800.

May 13th, 1861—This election passed with much less stir than for several years previous, owing to the excited state of the country at that time. The Board found the Association in a highly prosperous condition, but it is not to be expected that much progress will be made, during a time when all public institutions of this character must suffer more or less from the terrible consequences of the rebellion, which is menacing the very existence of the Government under which we live—a government, it should here be said, whose genius is to foster every enterprise of a peaceful and improving nature. It is not the intention of the Directors, however, to relax their efforts for the welfare and improvement of the Association, as the publication of this catalogue will sufficiently indicate. The large additions made to the list of newspapers and periodicals, is another evidence of their intention not to diminish the advantages and attractions offered by the Association; and it is earnestly to be hoped that the public support will not be withdrawn from an institution capable of exerting so large a degree of usefulness, and that nothing will occur to stay its advancement in the career of prosperity upon which it has now so fairly entered.

PAST OFFICERS.

A List of the Officers of the Young Men's Association, chosen at the different Elections, from December, 1847, to May, 1861:—

Elected December 20th and 27th, 1847.—President, J. H. VanDyke; Vice-Presidents, M. Mason and Joseph Curtis; Recording Secretary, J. L. McVickar; Corresponding Secretary, Rev. A. L. Chapin; Treasurer, S. Marshall; Trustees from the Honorary Members, B. McVickar, I. A. Lapham, E. Cramer, A. Finch, jr., and F. Randall; Junior Trustees, Hans Crocker and James Christie.

Elected January 19th, 1848.—The same officers, except that Edward Hopkins took the place of A. Finch, jr., and H. W. Tenney was elected Recording Secretary.

Elected January 18th, 1849. — President, S. O. Putnam; Vice-President, J. K. Bartlett; Treasurer, Sam. Marshall; Secretary, C. F. Ilsley; Trustees, B. McVickar, Edward Hopkins, I. A. Lapham, H. W. Tenney, Hans Crocker, F. Randall and A. F. Clarke.

Elected December 5th, 1849.—President, S. O. Putnam; Vice-President, Geo. LeFevre; Secretary, Chas. F. Ilsley; Treasurer, S. Marshall; Trustees, Edward Hopkins, B. McVickar, I. A. Lapham, H. W. Tenney, J. K. Bartlett, J. H. Tweedy and Robert Menzies.

Elected December 4th, 1850.—President, John P. McGregor; Vice-President, Robert O. Bradford; Treasurer, C. F. Ilsley; Secretary, Winfield Smith; Trustees, Robert Menzies, William J. Bell, A. McArthur, J. K. Bartlett, E. P. Allis, O. H. Waldo and Nelson McCracken.

Elected December 9th, 1851. — President. H. W. Tenney; Vice-President, M. J. Burke; Treasurer, W. J. Bell; Secretary, B. K. Miller; Trustees, Joshua Stark, J P. McGregor, H. J. Nazro, Winfield Smith, C. F. Ilsley, R. Menzies and J. K. Bartlett.

Elected October 5th, 1852.—President, R. Menzies; Vice-President, J. Stark; Treasurer, W. J. Bell; Secretary, J. R. Brigham; Trustees, W. H. Wright, A. Whittemore, B. B. Richards, A. Wilson, Wm. Hill, F. Baason and H. W. Tenney.

Elected October 5th, 1853.—President, J. K. Bartlett; Vice-President, J. R. Brigham; Treasurer, W. J. Bell; Secretary, J. D. Dunn; Trustees, A. F. Clarke, I. A. Lapham, Winfield Smith, W. H. Wright, B. W. Griswold, H. W. Tenney and R. Menzies.

Elected October 4th, 1854.—President, J. R. Brigham; Vice-President, C. F Ilsley; Treasurer, W. J. Bell; Secretary, I. N. Mason; Trustees, I. A. Lapham, Winfield Smith, N. S. Donaldson, George LeFevre, E. L. Buttrick, J. K. Bartlett and R. Menzies.

Elected May 2d, 1855.—President, J. R. Brigham; Vice-President, W. Smith; Treasurer, C. F. Ilsley; Secretary, I. N. Mason; Trustees, I. A. Lapham, C. J. Cary, George LeFevre, N. S. Donaldson, E. L. Buttrick, R. Menzies and J. K. Bartlett.

Elected May 7th, 1856.—President, J. R. Brigham; Vice-President, E. L. Buttrick; Treasurer, C. F. Ilsley; Secretary, C. A. Nazro; Trustees, I. A. Lapham, N. S. Donaldson, J. K. Bartlett, C. J. Cary, A. C. May, George LeFevre and W. H. Metcalf.

Elected May 1st, 1857.—President, J. R. Brigham; Vice-President, A. C. May; Treasurer, C. F. Ilsley; Secretary, C. A. Nazro; Trustees, I. A. Lapham, N. S. Donaldson, E. L. Buttrick, J. K. Bartlett, W. R. Freeman, W. H. Metcalf and C. J. Cary.

Elected May 5th, 1858.—President, A. C. May; Vice-President, N. C. Gridley; Treasurer, J. L. Spink; Secretary, W. G. Fitch; Trustees, F. H. Terry, E. W. Dennis, S. Edson, C. Caverno, W. Price, J. Johnston and J. P. Ilsley.

Elected May 5th, 1859.—President, J. P. Ilsley; Vice-President, C. Caverno; Treasurer, J. L. Spink; Secretary, J. MacAlister; Trustees, W. Price, J. Seville, O. E. Britt, H. C. Smith, D. McDonald, W. H. Jacobs and J. B. D. Cogswell.

Elected May 7th, 1860.—President, C. Caverno; Vice-President, J. B. D. Cogswell; Secretary, J. MacAlister; Treasurer, J. L. Spink; Trustees, O. E. Britt, W. L. Dana, F. W. Pitkin, E. E. Bowns, W. G. Fitch, D. Courtenay and F. S. Ilsley.

ACT OF INCORPORATION

OF THE

Young Men's Association

OF THE

CITY OF MILWAUKEE.

The People of the State of Wisconsin, represented in Senate and Assembly, do enact as follows:

SECTION 1. Henry W. Tenney, Martin J. Burke, Benj. K. Miller, Wm. J. Bell, John P. McGregor, John K. Bartlett, Charles F. Ilsley, Joshua Stark, Winfield Smith, Henry J. Nazro, Robert Menzies,their associates and successors, are hereby created a body corporate and politic, by the name of the Young Men's Association of the City of Milwaukee, and by that name to remain in perpetual succession for the purpose of establishing and maintaining a Library and Reading Room, instituting literary and scientific lectures, and providing other means of moral and intellectual improvement, with power for such purposes to take by purchase, devise or otherwise, and to hold, transfer and convey real and personal property to the amount of Twenty-five Thousand Dollars, and also, further to take, hold and convey, all such books, cabinets, library, furniture and apparatus, as may be necessary for attaining the objects, and carrying into effect the purposes of the said corporation.

SEC. 2. The control and disposal of the funds, property and estate, and the direction and management of all the concerns of the said corporation, under such directions and restrictions as may be imposed by the rules and regulations thereof, shall be vested in a Board of Directors, to consist of the President, Vice President, the Secretary, the Treasurer, and seven Trustees of said corporation, who shall be elected annually to their respective offices, by such members of the corporation not indebted thereto, as shall, by the rules and regulations thereof, be entitled to vote at such elections.

Sec. 3. The several officers of the said Association, at the time of the passage of this act, shall continue to hold their respective offices as officers of the corporation hereby created, until the expiration of the terms for which they were elected and qualified; and all personal property, funds or securities now owned and held by the said association, or by said officers, or either, or any of them, or by any other person or persons in trust for the said association, or for the use or benefit of the same, including all debts due, or to become due to the same from the members thereof, for stated dues in arrears, fines, &c., or from any other person or persons, shall vest in and become the property of, and may be sued for and recovered in the name of the corporation hereby created, and the said corporation shall assume and be liable for all the debts and obligations of said Association, contracted or incurred, and for all contracts and agreements entered into previous to the passage of this act, by any of the officers thereof lawfully acting in behalf of the said Association.

Sec. 4. The present Constitution and laws of the said Association, as far as the same are consistent with the provisions of this act, and not inconsistent with the Constitution or laws of this State, or of the United States, shall continue in force as the laws and regulations of the corporation hereby created, until the same shall be legally altered and amended, and it shall be the duty of the Board of Directors of the corporation hereby created, immediately after the passage of this act, to revise the existing Constitution and laws of the said Association, and prepare and perfect a complete code of rules and regulations for the government of the said corporation, and to present the same to the members of the said Association entitled to vote at a general meeting thereof, for their approval, and if the same be approved by a majority of all the members voting on the question of approval, they shall at once become the rules aud regulations of the said corporation, and the present Constitution and laws of said Association shall cease and be of no force or authority whatever, provided that notice of said meeting be given by publication in two newspapers in the City of Milwaukee, at least two weeks prior to said meeting, stating distinctly the time, place and object of said meeting, and provided further that a copy of the said rules and regulations shall be open to the inspection of the members of said Association at the Reading Room of the Association, at least one week previous to said meeting.

SEC. 5. The Board of Directors shall have power to fill vacancies in the several offices, and to appoint, and at pleasure remove such subordinate officers, agents or servants, as the business or interest of the said corporation may in their opinion require.

SEC. 6. The estate, property and funds of the said corporation, shall be devoted solely to the general purposes and objects specified in the first section of this act.

SEC. 7. This act shall take effect immediately.

J. McM. SHAFTER,
Speaker of the Assembly.

TIMOTHY BURNS,
President of the Senate.

Approved, March 8th, 1852.

LEONARD J. FARWELL,
Governor.

STATE OF WISCONSIN, } ss.
SECRETARY'S OFFICE. }

I, Charles D. Robinson, Secretary of State, of said State, having compared the foregoing law with the original deposited in this office, do hereby certify, that the same is a true copy thereof, and the whole of such original.

Witness my hand and the great seal of the State, at the Capitol, in Madison, this 27th day of March, 1852.

[L. S.]

CHARLES D. ROBINSON,
Secretary of State.

GENERAL RULES AND REGULATIONS

OF THE

Young Men's Association

OF THE

CITY OF MILWAUKEE.

ARTICLE I.

SECTION 1. Any person, if approved by any member of the Board of Directors, may become a member of the Association, by paying an initiation fee of one dollar, and one dollar for the dues of the next six months.

SEC. 2. Every member shall be subject to an annual assessment of two dollars, payable semi-annually in advance.

SEC. 3. Any person may become a life member of the Association, by the payment of twenty-five dollars in one sum, which shall entitle him to all the privileges of annual membership, without being subject to further dues.

SEC. 4. A membership of at least six months shall be requisite to make a member eligible to any office, after the election for 1859.

SEC. 5. Any member may withdraw from the Association, on paying up all dues and giving notice to the Librarian. The privileges of any member shall be suspended during his neglect to pay dues or fines, and a continuance of such neglect for one year, shall forfeit his membership, unless his delinquencies shall be excused by the Board of Directors.

SEC. 6. There shall be a meeting of the members of the Association on the first Tuesday in May of each year, for the purpose of receiving the reports of the Board of Directors, and the Treasurer, and for the transaction of such other business connected with the affairs of the Association, as may be presented for consideration Notice of the time and place of which meeting shall be given, at least ten days prior to its being held, in one or more of the public newspapers of the city.

SEC. 7. Special meetings of the members of the Association may be called by the President, when requested to do so by any four members of the Board of Directors, or any ten members of the Association, in writing, and the same notice of such special meeting shall be given, as is required by the preceeding section, for the annual meeting, and no other business shall be transacted at any such special meeting, than shall be named in the call.

ARTICLE II. — OF OFFICERS.

SECTION 1. The officers of the Association, as prescribed in the Act of Incorporation, shall consist of a President, Vice-President, Secretary, Treasurer, and seven Trustees, all of whom shall be elected annually, by ballot, on a general ticket, and a plurality of the votes cast, shall be necessary to constitute an election.

SEC. 2. It shall be the duty of the President to preside at all meetings of the Association and Board of Directors, preserve order therein, appoint all committees not otherwise provided for, and in case of an equal division of the members on any question, give the casting vote. He shall also, at the annual meeting of the Association, appoint three inspectors to superintend the next election of officers.

SEC. 3. In case of the death or absence of the President, or his inability to act, the Vice-President shall perform the duties of the office, and in case of the absence or inability of both the President and Vice-President, some person to be appointed by the Board of Directors, shall perform the duties of the office for the time being.

SEC. 4. The Secretary shall keep an accurate record of the transactions of the Association and of the Board of Directors, shall notify officers of their election, give notice of the meetings of the Association, and of the Board, and perform all other duties usually incident to that office.

SEC. 5. The Treasurer shall receive and safely keep all moneys of the Association, and pay them out only on the order of the Board of Directors, upon drafts on him issued by the Secretary, and countersigned by the President. He shall keep an accurate account of all receipts and disbursements, report the same to the Board of Directors, whenever required, and also to the Association at each annual meeting, together with the vouchers in support of the same. He shall, within ten days after receiving notice of his election, and before entering upon the duties of his office, execute a bond to the Association, with two sureties, to be approved by the Board of Directors, in such sum as the Board shall direct, conditioned for the faithful performance of his duties.

SEC. 6. The Board of Directors, consisting of all of the foregoing officers, shall have the control and management of the affairs and property of the Association, and shall institute such By-Laws and Regulations, not inconsistent with these general Rules and Regulations, and the Act of Incorporation, as may seem from time to time necessary for attaining the objects and carrying into effect the purposes of this Association. They shall at each annual meeting report to the Association, by the President, a full account of their transactions during the preceding year, and give a statement of the condition of the Library and state of the Association.

SEC. 7. A Librarien shall be appointed by the Board of Directors, who shall, under their supervision, take charge of the Rooms and of the Library, and other property of the Association. He shall keep a register of all Books, Maps, Charts, and other property belonging to the Association, (with the names of donors, in cases where books or articles have been presented,) arrange them in proper order, and perform such other services as may be required of him from time to time by the Board of Directors.

SEC. 8. The Board of Directors shall meet on the Tuesday evening succeeding their election, for the purpose of organization; and thereafter, they shall meet at least once in each month. They shall also meet on the Tuesday following the next annual election, to receive the report of the Inspectors of Election.

SEC. 9. The Board of Directors shall have power to fill all vacancies occurring in their number.

SEC. 10. If the officers in their several official capacities, shall neglect the performance of their duties, or shall not administer the laws of the Association efficiently and equitably, on written complaint of twenty members, a meeting shall be called and a committee appointed, consisting of two members and one director, who shall report and refer the subject to the Association, and they shall censure, remove from office, or exonerate the accused, as the circumstances of the case may warrant.

ARTICLE III. — ELECTION.

SECTION 1. The annual election of officers of the Association shall be held on the Monday following the first Tuesday in May, of each year ; notice of which election shall be given in the same manner, and at the same time with the notice for the annual meeting.

SEC. 2. The election shall be held under the superintendence of three Inspectors, previously appointed, and the polls shall be kept open from two o'clock P. M., to nine o'clock P. M.

SEC. 3. A list of all members of the Association shall be furnished the Inspectors by the Librarian, stating if any dues are unpaid, and the amount; and no person shall be allowed to vote, who is in arrears for dues.

SEC. 4. The Inspectors of Election shall report to the Board of Directors, on the Tuesday following the annual election, the result of said election, and on receiving the said report, duly certified and accompanied by proof, that the notice of such election was duly given, as required by the Rules and Regulations, the Board of Directors shall order the report to be placed on the Records of the Association, when the several persons elected shall be deemed qualified for their several offices and notice of their election shall be given to them by the Secretary.

ARTICLE IV. — ALTERATIONS AND AMENDMENTS.

SECTION 1. These Rules and Regulations may be altered or amended by a vote of two-thirds of the members present at any meeting of the Association, provided such proposed alteration or amendment has been submitted to the Board of Directors, at a meeting of said Board, at least two weeks before action upon the same, and provided notice of the nature and substance of the proposed alteration or amendment be duly published, with notice of the meeting at which the same is to be acted upon, and a full copy of said proposed alteration or amendment is left with the Librarian for the inspection of any member, at least two weeks before the said meeting.

RULES AND REGULATIONS

OF

The Board of Directors.

1. Regular meetings of the Board shall be held on the first Monday evening of every month, at 7½ o'clock, at the Rooms of the Association; and also on the Tuesday evening, next after the general election.

2. Special meetings may be called at any time by the President, or in his absence or other inability, by any two members of the Board.

3. Notice of all meetings shall be given to each member, by a note from the Secretary, which may be left at the usual place of business or abode of the member, or deposited in the post-office, addressed to him.

4. Six members of the Board shall constitute a quorum for the transaction of business, though a less number may adjourn a meeting from time to time, or *sine die.*

5. After any meeting shall have been called to order, general conversation shall not be allowed, and any member speaking, shall address the presiding officer, who shall assign to him the floor for that purpose, and he shall confine himself to the question before the Board.

6. The order of business, at all meetings of the Board, shall be: 1st. Reading of the journal of the last meeting. 2d. Presentation of accounts, petitions, reports of committees, &c. 3d. Introduction of resolutions, &c. 4th. Any business, not included under the foregoing, that may come before the Board.

7. All resolutions offered for the consideration of the Board, shall be in writing, endorsed with the name of the member intro-

ducing the same; and all motions, when desired by any member, shall be presented in the same manner.

8. The Standing Committees of the Board, to consist of three members each, shall be a Committee on Library and Reading Room, Committee on Finance, and a Committee on Lectures.

9. The several Standing Committees shall make a written report of their doings to the Board at the meetings held on the first Monday of the months of February, May, August and November, and at such other times as the Board may require.

10. These rules may be altered at any meeting, by a vote of two-thirds of the members of the Board, or suspended by a vote of two-thirds of the members present.

RULES

OF THE

Library and Reading Room.

LIBRARY.

Rule 1. The Library shall be open for the delivery and return of books, every day, (Sundays and holidays excepted,) from nine A. M. to twelve M., from two to five, and from seven to nine o'clock P. M.

Rule 2. The Librarian shall see that the books, library and reading room are kept in good order; shall keep a full and accurate catalogue of all the books, pamphlets, maps, charts, newspapers and works of art belonging to the Association, and arrange them in proper order, which catalogue, or a duplicate thereof, shall at all times be open to the inspection of the members. He shall make a record of all books, maps, charts, works of art, &c., presented to the Association, in a book provided for that purpose, with the names of the donors.

Rule 3. He shall, under the direction of the Library Committee, keep account of all books delivered and returned, all damage and loss of books, all dues of members, and all fines and penalties incurred.

Rule 4. He shall collect all dues, all fines and penalties incurred by the members, and account for the same to the Treasurer on the first Monday of the months of May, August, November and February, and at such other times as the Board of Directors may require.

Rule 5. He shall, at the times above specified, or oftener, if required by the Board of Directors, report to them the amount of dues, fines or forfeitures, at such times remaining unpaid, with the names of those members who may neglect or refuse to pay their dues, fines or forfeitures, and the amount respectively due from each; the names of such members as may lose or damage any book or other property of the Association, accompanied by an assessment of such loss or damage, and of such as have not returned upon due notice, as provided for by rule 6, the books taken by them from the library, with the titles of such books.

RULE 6. He shall on the first Monday of the months of April, July, October and January, notify each member who has not then returned in due season, the book or books, by such member taken from the library, of such default, and require the return thereof forthwith.

RULE 7. No person shall be allowed the privileges of the Library or Reading Room while indebted to the Association for any dues or penalties.

RULE 8. Every member may draw from the Library one volume, octavo, or two volumes of less size, if connected and belonging to one set.

RULE 9. No book shall be detained longer than two weeks, unless renewed; and if detained longer, the person detaining the same shall pay for every week's detention, ten cents; one day's detention over a week being considered equivalent to a full week.

RULE 10. All books may be renewed for one week, except such books as shall have been added to the library within one year previous to the time of application for renewal. After the return of any book, the same person shall not take the same volume again, till it has remained in the library two full days.

RULE 11. Every member shall be responsible for loss or injury of any book or set drawn by him; the damage to be assessed by the Librarian; provided that the member may appeal from the decision of the Librarian to the Board of Directors.

RULE 12. Any member may introduce any person, not a resident of the city, to the rooms of the Association, entering his own name with that of the person introduced by him, upon a book provided for that purpose. The person so introduced shall be entitled to the privileges of the Library and Reading Room for one month, but shall not be privileged to take books, pamphlets or papers from the rooms of the Association.

RULE 13. Books marked in the catalogue as books of reference, and such others as may from time to time be specially designated by the Board, shall not be taken from the Library, except by special permission of the Board of Directors.

RULE 14. Smoking or conversation in the Library or Reading Rooms is prohibited.

RULE 15. Any person who shall misplace any book upon the shelves of the Library, shall pay a fine of ten cents for each book so misplaced.

RULE 16. The Rules of the Library and Reading Room may be altered or amended at any time, by the Board of Directors.

READING ROOM.

RULE 1. The Reading Room shall be open every day, (Sundays excepted,) from half past seven o'clock A. M., to ten o'clock P. M.

RULE 2. The Librarian shall take charge of the Reading Room, and keep in their places, all the books, periodicals and newspapers belonging therein, and shall enforce such rules and regulations for the government of this department as the Board may enact.

RULE 3. The last number of each quarterly, monthly, weekly and daily periodical, shall be kept on the table or the files of the Reading Room. Earlier numbers may be taken from the Reading Room by permission of the Librarian, for one week only, subject to a fine of ten cents per week, if kept longer than that time.

RULE 4. None but members and such as have been introduced, as provided by Library Rule No. 12, shall be allowed the privileges of the Reading Room.

RULE 5. Any person who shall mutilate the periodicals or papers placed in the Reading Room, or remove them therefrom, shall be liable to a fine equal to four times the cost thereof.

PERIODICALS AND NEWSPAPERS.

DAILY.

Milwaukee Sentinel, (gratuitous)
" News, "
" Free Democrat, "
" Wisconsin, "
" Daily Life, "
St. Louis Democrat,
Chicago Tribune,
" Post,
Cincinnati Gazette,

London Times,
New York Times,
" Herald,
" Tribune,
" World,
Boston Journal,
Philadelphia Press,
Toronto Globe,
Madison ——, during Session.

TRI-WEEKLY.—Cleveland Plaindealer.

SEMI-WEEKLY.—Albany Atlas & Argus.

WEEKLY.

Louisville Journal,
New York Independent,
Living Age,
Rebellion Record,

Manitowoc Herald, (gratuitous,)
Prescott Transcript, "
Hartford Press,
Springfield Republican,

Publishers' Circular.

ILLUSTRATED WEEKLIES.

London News,
" Punch,
Vanity Fair,

Harpers Weekly,
New York Mercury,
New York Ledger,

Scientific American.

MONTHLY.

The Knickerbocker,
The Atlantic,
Harper's,
The Crayon,
Hunt's Merchants',

Blackwood's,
The Cornhill,
Temple Bar,
Chambers' Journal,
All The Year Round.

BI-MONTHLY.—Silliman's Journal.

QUARTERLY.

London Quarterly Review,
Edinburgh Review,
North British Review,
Westminster Review,
North American Review,
Church Review,
Methodist Quarterly,
Christian Review,
Bibliotheca Sacra,
Brownson's Quarterly,
Christian Examiner.

MAPS.

Colton's Map of the World, (mounted.)
Colton's Map of the United States, (mounted.)
Maury's Map of the United States, "
Lapham's Map of Wisconsin, two dates, "
Chapman's Map of Wisconsin, "
Lapham's Map of Milwaukee, "
Lapham's Map of Milwaukee, (pocket form.)
Bird's-Eye View of the Seat of War, 1861.
Colton's European Battle-Fields, 1854.
125 Maps, Charts, &c., chiefly published under the direction of Coast Survey and War Departments.

NEWSPAPERS OF EARLY DATES, &c.

Newport Mercury, December 19, 1758.
New Haven Gazette, July 17, 1788.
American Mercury, February to December, 1796.
Ulster County Gazette, January 4, 1800.
Philadelphia Portfolio, September 19, 1801.
Philadelphia Gazette, January 26, 1803.
Federal Republican, June 9, 1815.
London Courier, February 7, 1820.
London True Briton, November 4, 1820.
Bill of Convent Garden Theatre, July 18, 1821.
"The King and Canning, his Game-Cock ;" ballad, published at the period.
Note for £1 on the Colony of Pennsylvania, 1773.
China newspapers, &c., &c.

Catalogue.

F

EXPLANATORY NOTE.

It will aid the reader in the use of the following catalogue, to bear in mind, that this is not a *classified* catalogue, nor technically speaking, a *descriptive* catalogue, neither does it attempt to furnish the popular designation of Books,—about which there would probably be no uniform agreement.

The plan adopted has been, firstly, to place each work, alphabetically, under the name, if known, or *nom de plume* of the *author, editor or translator* (making the proper distinction in the latter cases) ; and, secondly, under its literal *title*, or, if abridged, to do so as nearly as possible in the words of the original. *On the shelves,* the Books are arranged numerically, and classified according to subject.

Consideration of size and price, has compelled the abridgment of lengthy titles of Books, and the omission of all personal titles, unless essential parts of names, or when used by way of explanation, when the christian names are not known, and to distinguish authors having the same initials.

For volumes of "Executive Documents" wholly devoted to one subject, the reader is referred to the letters to which their specific titles respectively belong ; and, for late volumes of Reports originally published in separate form, to the "Executive" or "Miscellaneous" Documents of subsequent years.

The *subject* of a memoir or life, is not necessarily to be found under the appropriate letter, except the work is partially or altogether autobiographical.

Books without an acknowledged or attributed authorship, can, of course, only be found in the "Catalogue by titles."

*** Provision has been made in the numbering for future additions to the several departments.

CATALOGUE

OF THE LIBRARY OF THE

Young Men's Association

OF THE

CITY OF MILWAUKEE.

PART I.—BY AUTHORS.

Abbott, B. V. & L. (Benauly)—Cone Cut Corners . 5727

—— —— —— Matthew Caraby . . 3204

—— J. S. C.—Empire of Austria 546

—— —— Empire of Russia 528

—— —— French Revolution 157

—— —— History of N. Bonaparte . . 873–4

—— —— Italy 529

—— —— South and North 1902

Abercrombie, J.—Inquiries Concerning the Intellectual Powers 3083

—— — Philosophy of the Moral Feelings . 3082

About, E.—King of the Mountains, The . . . 4629

—— — Roman Question, The 2254

Adams —Sable Cloud, The 4639

—— Mrs.—Daily Duties 3863

—— F. C.—Justice in the By-Ways 4631

—— J.—Letters of 1317–18

—— — Works of 2099–2108

—— Mrs. J.—Letters of 1360

—— J. Q.—Letters on Masonry 2977

Adams, J. T (?)—Lost Hunter 5732
——— J. W. (Ed'r)—Appleton's Mechanics' Magazine, vol. i. 5966
——— —— —— Appleton's Mechanics' Magazine, vols. ii.–iii. 7723–4
Addison, J. et al.—Spectator, The 3555
Æsop—Fables 3718
Agassiz, L.—Contributions to the N. History of the U. States. Vols. i.–iii. 7695–7
——— — Lake Superior 1591
——— — and Gould, A. A.—Principles of Zoology 2361
Aguilar, Grace—Days of Bruce, The 4632–3
——— —— Home Influence 4637
——— —— Home Scenes 4634
——— —— Mother's Recompense 4638
——— —— Vale of Cedars, The 4635
——— —— Woman's Friendship 4636
——— —— Women of Israel 3122–3
Aikin, J.—Letters to his Son 3851
——— Lucy—Life of J. Addison 1120
——— —— Memoirs of J. Aikin 842
——— —— Memoirs of the Court of Charles I. 111–12
——— —— Memoirs of the Court of Elizabeth . 119–20
——— —— Memoirs of the Court of James I. . 117–18
Ainsworth, W. H.—Old St. Paul's 4627
——— —— Tower of London 4626
Akenside, M.—Poetical Works of 4080
Alcott, W. A.—Young Man's Guide 3865
Aldrich, T. B.—Ballad of Babie Belle 4085
——— —— Pampinea, &c. 4089
Alger, W. R.—Poetry of the East 4079
Alison, Sir A.—History of Europe, '89–'15 . . . 60–3
——— —— History of Europe, '15–'52 . . . 64–72
——— —— Military Life of the Duke of Marlborough 1102
——— —— Miscellaneous Essays 3550
Allen, D. O.—India 384
—— P.—History of Lewis and Clarke's Expedition . 1961–2
—— W.—American Biographical Dictionary . . 7909

Blair, F. P, et al, (Ed'rs)—Con. Globe i S. xxvii C. 7497

———— " " ii S. xxix C. 7502

———— " " ii S. xxx C. 7505

———— " " i S. xxxi C. &Ap. 7506-9

———— " " ii S. xxxi C. 7510

———— " " i S. xxxii C. " 7511-14

———— " " ii S. xxxii C. " 7518

———— " " i S. xxxiii C. " 7519-22

———— " " ii S. xxxiii C. " 7523-4

———— " " i S. xxxiv C. " 7525-8

———— " " iii S. xxxiv C. " 7533-4

———— " " i S. xxxv C. " 7535-8

—— H.—Lectures on Rhetoric 2972

—— R. et al.—Selections from the British Classics 4116

Blake, J. L.—Family Encyclopædia . . . 7886

—— W. O.—History of Slavery . . . 2047

Blanc, L.—History of Ten Years . . . 170--1

—— — History of the French Revolution, vol. i. 165

Blessington, Lady—Journal of Coversations with Byron 1128

Blodget, L.—Climatology of the United States . 2312

Boccacio, G.—Decameron, The 3233

Bogart, W. H.—Daniel Boone and the Hunters of Kentucky 1328

Bohn, H. G.—Catalogue of Books, 1831 . . . 3999

Boismont, A. B. de—Hallucinations . . . 2324

Boker, G. H.—Plays and Poems 4445-6

Bolinbroke, Lord—Works of 2983-6

Bonaparte, Lucien—Memoirs of 1231

———— N.—Confidential Correspondence with his Brother 1226-7

Bonar, A. R.—Life of the Duke of Wellington . . 1452

Borrow, G.—Bible in Spain, The 1566

Boswell, J.—Life of S. Johnson 824-5

Botta, C.—History of the War of Independence . 223-4

Boussingault, J. B.—Rural Economy . . . 2504

Bouterwek, F.—History of Spanish Literature . 3324

Boyd, A. K. H. (?)—Recreations of a Country Parson 3216

Boyer, A.—French Dictionary 7894

Brace, C. L.—Hungary in '51 1699

Bradford, A.—History of Massachusetts . . . 308

Bradford, W. J. A.—Notes on the North-West . . 578
Brady, W.—Kedge-Anchor 2529
Brainard, J. G. C.—Poems 4115
Brande, J.—Observations on Popular Antiquities . 462–4
——— W. T.—Dictionary of Science, Literature and Art 7895
Bremer, Miss F.—Diary, A, H—— Family, &c. . . 4689
——— ——— Father and Daughter (2 copies) 4690–1
——— ——— Home, The, &c. 4692
——— ——— Homes in the New World . . 1835-6
——— ——— Life in the Old World . . . 1639–40
——— ——— Neighbors, The, &c., (2 copies) . 4693–5
——— ——— President's Daughters, The . . 4696
Brewster, Anne M. H.—Compensation . . . 4699
——— Sir D.—Life of Sir I. Newton, (H. F. L.) 1446
——— ——— Martyrs of Science . . . 1430
——— ——— Memoirs of Sir I. Newton . . 846–7
——— ——— et al.—Encyclop. Britan. vol. i.–xxi. 7763–83
——— ——— " " Sup. to vol. i. 7785
Briggs, C. F., and Maverick, A.—Story of the Telegraph 2539
Brodhead, J. R.—History of New York . . . 284
Bronte, Anne—Tenant of Wildfell Hall (2 copies) . 4710-11
——— Charlotte—Jane Eyre (2 copies) . . . 4712-13
——— ——— Professor, The . . . 4714
——— ——— Shirley 4715
——— ——— Villette 4716
——— Emily Jane—Wuthering Heights, (2 copies) . 4717-18
Brookes, J.—Manners and Customs of the English 3668
Brooks, Shirley—Aspen Court 4721
——— ——— Silver Cord, The - . . . 5792
Broom, H.—Selection of Legal Maxims . . . 2172
Brougham, J.—Humorous Stories 4698
——— L'd—Discourses of Natural Theology . 2847
——— — Historical Sketches of Statesmen . 949-50
——— — Lives of Men of Letters . . . 948
——— — Political Philosophy . . . 2018-20
——— — Speeches 3938-9
——— — et al.—Discourse on the Adv. and Plea. of Science, &c. 2325

Carlyle, T.—Heroes, Hero-Worship, &c. . . . 3125
——— — History of Frederick II., vols. i.-ii. . 1278-9
——— — Life of F. Schiller 1275
——— — Life of J. Sterling 1134
——— — Sartor Resartus, &c. 3124
——— — (Ed'r)—Oliver Cromwell's Letters & Speeches 1108-9
Carnes, J. A.—Journal of a Voyage to Africa . 1805
Carpenter, W. B.—Microscope, The 2413
Cary, H.—Memorials of the Civil War . . 103-4
—— H. F.—Lives of the Poets 954
Cassin, J.—Illustrations of North American Birds 2313
Catherine II.—Memoirs of 1295
Catlin, J.—Illustrations of the Manners, &c. of the N. A. Indians 349-50
Cellini, B.—Memoirs of 1301
Cervantes, M. de.—Don Quixote 5820-1
——— —— El Buscapie 3210
——— —— Exemplary Novels of . . 4831
Chalmers, T.—Adaptation of External Nature (Br. Trea.) 2853
——— — Lectures on the Epistle to the Romans 2720
——— — Miscellanies 2719
——— — Sermons 2721-2
Chamberlayne, J.—Magnæ Britanniae Notitia (1745) 465
Chambers, R. (?)—Vestiges of the Natural Hist. of Creation 2349
——— — (Ed'r)—Cyclopædia of Eng. Literature 7870-1
——— W.—Chambers' Miscellany 3382-91
——— W. & R. (Ed'rs)—Edinburgh Journal, vols. xvii.-xx. . 7109-11
——— ——— —— Edinburgh Journal, vols. i.-xiv., N. S. . 7112-20
——— ——— —— Information for the People 7872-3
Chandler, D. H.—Rep. of the Sup. C't of Wis. vols. i.-iv. 8810-12
——— P. W.—American Criminal Trials . 2268-9
Channing, W. E.—Memoir of 1391-3
——— —— Works of 2811-16
Chanter, Charlotte—Over the Cliffs 4829
Chapman, G. W.—Tribute to Kane, &c. . . . 4125
——— S.—Hand Book of Wisconsin . 584
Chaptal, J. A.—Chemistry applied to Agriculture 2466

Chateaubriand, F. A. de—Genius of Christianity . 2690
——— ——— Martyrs, The . . . 4528
——— ——— Recollections of Italy . . 1567
Chatham, L'd., et al.—Celebrated Speeches of . . 3919
Chatterton, T.—Poetical Works of 4127–8
Chatto, W. A.—Facts and Speculations on the History of Cards 3815
Chaucer, G.—Poetical Works of 4034
Cheever, G. B.—Wanderings in the Shadow of Mount Blanc 1707
——— H. T.—Island World of the Pacific . . 1929
——— ——— Reel in a Bottle, A 4481
Chesterfield, L'd.—Works of 3584
Chevalier, M.—Probable Fall in the Value of Gold . 2198
Child, F. J. (Ed'r)—English and Scottish Ballads . 4117–24
——— Mrs. L. M.—Isaac T. Hopper, A True Life . 1398
——— ——— Memoirs of Mesdames De Stael and Roland 1072
——— ——— Philothea 4830
——— ——— Progress of Religious Ideas . 2807–9
Choules, J. O.—Cruise of the North Star . . 1645
Churchill, C.—Poetical Works of 4134–6
Cicero, M. T.—De Officiis, etc. 4022
——— ——— Orations, Offices, &c. 3940–2
Clark, L. G.—Knick-Knacks 3235
——— W. G. and L. G. (Ed'rs)—Knickerbocker Magazine, The vols. xxxiv.–lvii. . . . 7261–84
Clarke, J. F.—Eleven Weeks in Europe . . 1632
——— Mrs. M. C.—Complete Concordance to Shakspeare 7876
——— ——— Iron Cousin, The (2 copies) . 4850–1
Clay H.—Life, Correspondence and Speeches of . 2119–24
Cler, (Gen.)—Reminiscences of an Officer of Zouaves 1651
Clive, Lady—Paul Ferroll 5736
Cluskey, M. W.—Political Text Book 2042
Cobbett, W.—History of the English Reformation . 2782
Cockburn, L'd—Life of L'd Jeffrey 1171–2
——— — Memorials of his Time . . . 1103
Cockton, H.—Lady Felicia 4834

Elder, W.—Biography of E. K. Kane, ... 929
Eliot, S.—History of Liberty—Ancient Romans . 2049-50
—— — " " Early Christians . 2051-2
—— W. G., Jr.—Lectures to Young Men . 3862
—— —— — " " Women . 3861
Ellet, C., Jr.—Con. to the Phys. Geo. of U. S.—Miss. Valley 7710
—— Mrs. E. F.—Domestic History of the Revolution 567
—— —— —— Women Artists 3610
Elliott, C. W.—New England History . . . 277-8
Ellis, G.—Specimens of Metrical Romances, . . 3203
—— W. Polynesian Researches 1925-8
Emerson, G.—American Farmer's Encyclopædia, The 2476
—— J. Letters from the Ægean . . . 1604
—— R. W.—Conduct of Life, (2 copies) . 3315-16
—— —— English Traits 1654
—— —— Essays 3344-5
—— —— Miscellanies 3328
—— —— Poems 4168
—— —— Representative Men 3166
Emory, W. H.—Notes of a Military Reconnoisance 1522
—— —— et al.—Report of the Mexican Boundary Survey 7439-41
Ennemoser, J.—History of Magic 3060-1
Erving, J. F. et al.—Milwaukee City Directory, 1857-8 2212
Espy, J. P.—Meteorological Report, ii., and iv. . 7448, 7450
Euler, L.—Letters on Natural Philosophy . 2457-8
Evans, T.—Walks through Wales 1682
Everett, E.—Importance of Education . . 3801
—— — Life of Geo. Washington . . . 1315
—— — Mt. Vernon Papers 3169
—— — Orations and Speeches 3914-16
—— — et al.—Obituary Address on the death of W. R. King 924
Evans, Miss A. J.—Beulah (2 copies) . . . 4987-8
—— Miss M. (George Eliot)—Adam Bede . 4989
—— —— —— Mill on the Floss (2 copies) 4990-1
—— —— —— Silas Marner . 4992-3
Ewbank, T.—Desc. & Hist. Acc. of Hydraulic Machines 2530
—— — Life in Brazil 1601

Francis, G. H.—Orators of the Age 3153
Franklin, B.—Memoirs of 1475-6
——— — Works of 2089-98
Fraser, J. B.—Hist. and Des. Account of Persia . 738
—— —— Mesopotamia and Assyria . . 739
Freedley, E. T.—Practical Treatise on Business . 2229
Fremont, J. C.—Exploring Expedition to Oregon, &c. 1856
——— —— Narrative of the Expl'ng Expedition, 1842 1857
——— —— Report of the Exploring " 1520
French, W. H., et al.—Instructions for Field Artillery 2543
Froebel, J.—Seven Years in Central America . 1597
Froissart, J.—Chronicles of England, France, &c. 54
Frost, J.—Border Wars 348
—— — Indian Wars of the United States . 352
—— — (Ed'r)—Select British Poets—Falconer to Scott 4042
—— ——— " " " Southey to Croly 4043
Fuller, R., and Wayland F.—Domestic Slavery . 3086
Fullerton, Lady G.—Ellen Middleton . . 5026
——— ——— Grantley Manor . . . 5027
——— ——— Lady Bird . . . 5028
Furness, W. H.—Thoughts on Jesus . . . 2858
Gales, J., et al. (Ed'r)—An. of Congress, 1789-1824 8022-63
Galligher, W. D. —— Hesperian, The, vol. ii. . 5965
Galt, J.—Laurie Todd 5048
—— — Life of L'd Byron 1449
—— — " T. Wolsey 1389
—— — Sir Andrew Wylie 5049
Gangooly, J. C.—Life and Religion of the Hindoos . 2817
Gardner, A. K.—Old Wine in New Bottles . . 1686
Garland, H. A.—Life of J. Randolph 928
Garrick, D., et al.—British Drama 4416–17
Gaskell, Mrs. E. C.—Life of Charlotte Bronte . . 1167–8
——— ——— Ruth 5054
Gautier, T.—Wanderings in Spain 1709
Gay, J.—Poetical Works of 4185–6
Gayarre, C.—History of Louisiania 310
Genlis, M'me de—Lessons of a Governess . . 3802–3
George, Anita—Annals of the Queens of Spain . 1017–18
Gerard (the Lion Killer)—Adventures of . . 1819

Gerstæcker, F.—Wanderings of German Emigrants . 1837
Gibbon, E.—History of Rome 35–8
—— L.—Exploration of the Amazon, with Maps . 1528–9
Gibbs, G.—Memoirs of the Federal Administrations 225–6
Giddings, J. R.—Exiles of Florida. . . . 3661
Giles, H.—Christian Thought on Life . . . 2913
—— — Illustrations of Genius 3149
—— — Lectures and Essays, vol. ii . . . 3341
Gilfillan, G.—Sketches of Literature, vol. i . . 3138
Gillespie, W. M.—Manual of Road Making . . 2528
Gillies, J.—History of the World 3–5
—— — Memoirs and Sermons of G. Whitefield . 850
Gilliss, J. M.—U. S. Naval Astronom. Exp'ns vols. i–iii 7405–7
—— —— " " " vol. vi 7410
Gleig, G. R.—History of the Bible . . . 2938–9
Goadby, H.—Text-Book of Physiology . . . 2298
Goddard, Miss A. A.—Gleanings 3197
Godwin, P.—History of France, vol. i . . . 151
—— — (Ed'r)—Hand-Book of Univ. Biography 7916
—— W.—St. Leon 5064
—— — Things as They Are (Caleb Williams) . 4616–17
Goethe, J. W. von—Correspondence with a Child . 3129
—— —— Dramatic Works of . . 4439
—— —— Faust 4181
—— —— Hermann and Dorothea . . 4182
—— —— Poems and Ballads . . . 4183
—— —— Truth and Poetry from my own Life 1268–9
—— —— Wilhelm Meister . . . 5055–6
—— —— et al.—Sorrows of Werter, &c. . 4604
—— —— and Schiller, F.—Select Minor Poems 4180
Goldsmith, O.—Poetical Works of 4187
—— — Works of 3392–5
Goodrich, C. A.—Elements of Greek Grammar . 4019
—— —— Select British Eloquence . . 3913
—— S. G.—Attache in Madrid . . . 1710
—— —— Recollections of a Lifetime . . 1344–5
—— F. B.—Man Upon the Sea 1602
Goodwin, P. A.—Biography of A. Jackson . . 1331
Gordon, T. F.—Digest of U. S. Laws . . . 2173

Halleck, Fitz-Green—Poetical Works . . 4057

—— —— (Ed'r)—Selections from British Poets 4383-4

—— H. W.—Elements of Military Art . . 2542

Halsted, Caroline A.—Richard III. 812

Hamilton, A., et al.—Federalist, The . . . 2053

—— S.—History of the U. S. Flag . . 3660

—— —— T.—Cyril Thornton 5112

—— Sir W.—Lectures on Logic . . 2970

—— —— Lectures on Metaphysics . . 2961

—— —— Philosophy of . . . 2967

Hamley, (Capt.)—Lady Lee's Widowhood . . 5840

Hammond, S. H.—Hills, Lake and Forest Streams . 1850

Hanna, W.—Memoirs of Chalmers . . . 1399-1402

Hare, Brothers—Guesses at Truth 3317

Harland, Marion—Alone 5118

—— —— Nemesis (2 copies) . . . 5116–17

Harris, J.—Man Primeval 2850

—— —— Pre-Adamite Earth 2849

—— W. C.—Adventures in Africa . . . 1511

Harrison, H. W.—Battle-Fields 341

Hatfield, R. G.—American House-Carpenter . . 2526

Hawks, F. L.—Monuments of Egypt . . . 386

Hawker, P.—Instructions to Young Sportsmen . . 3819

—— —— Narrative of the Japan Expedition . 1492

—— —— et al.—Coll'ns N. Y. Hist. So., vol. iii, part i. 3963

—— —— —— Nar. of the U. S. Japan Expedition—(Gov. ed.) . . . 7420–2

Hawthorne, N.—Blithedale Romance 5091

—— —— House of Seven Gables, The . 5082

—— —— Marble Faun (2 copies) . . . 5084–7

—— —— Mosses from an Old Manse . . 3255

—— —— Scarlet Letter, The 5088

—— —— Tanglewood Tales 4603

—— —— Twice-Told Tales 5089–90

—— —— (Ed'r)—Journal of an African Cruiser 1820

Hayes, I. I.—Arctic Boat Journey 1941

Hazen, D. A.—Five Years Before the Mast . . 1937

—— E.—Popular Technology 2552–3

Hazlitt, W.—Lectures on Dramatic Literature . . 3157

——— — Lectures on the Comic Writers . . 3156

——— — Life of N. Bonaparte 1218–21

——— — Spirit of the Age 3155

——— — Table Talk 3158–9

Head, Sir F. B.—Bubbles from the Brunnen . . 1700

——— ——— Faggot of French Sticks . . 1683

——— ——— Life of J. Bruce . . . 1440

Headley, J. T.—Adirondack, The 3893

——— ——— Letters from Italy 1728

——— ——— Life of O. Cromwell 1110

——— ——— Life of Havelock 1117

——— ——— Life of Winfield Scott . . . 1323

——— ——— Napoleon and his Marshals . . 1015–16

——— P. C.—Life of Josephine 1228

Heber, R.—Narrative of a Journey through India . 1777–8

——— —Poetical Works of 4051

Heck, J. G. (Ed'r)—Iconographic Encyclopædia . 7862–7

Hedge, F. H. (Ed'r)—Prose Writers of Germany . 3499

Helps, A.—Friends in Council 3333-4

——— — Spanish Conquest in America . . . 538-40

Helper, H. R.—Impending Crisis, The . . . 2255

Hemans, Mrs. F.—Poetical Works of 4054

Henry, C. S.—Doctor Oldham at Greystones . . 3217

——— ——— Epitome of the History of Philosophy 3076-7

——— J. et al—Annual Report of the Smithsonian Institution, 1853-7 8624-8

——— P. et al.—American Oratory 3918

——— W. S.—Campaign Sketches 606

Hentz, Caroline L.—Courtship and Marriage . . 5119

Herbert, G.—Poetical Works of 4204

——— H. W.—Captains of the Roman Republic . 3145

——— ——— Cavaliers of England . . . 5113

——— ——— Complete Manual for Y. Sportsmen 3830

——— ——— Frank Forester's Field Sports . 3822-3

——— ——— Sporting Scenes 3832-3

Herndon, (Lieut.)—Explor. of the Amazon, with Maps 1526-7

Heroditus—History 410

Herrick, R.—Hesperides, &c. 4205-6

Hood, F. F. B., and T. (Ed'rs)—Memorials of T. Hood 1148-9
—— T.—Hood's Own 3637
—— — Poems 4200-3
—— — Tylney Hall 5071
—— — Up the Rhine 3635-6
—— — Whims and Waifs 4199
—— — Whimsicalities 3638
Hook, T.—All in the Wrong 5100
—— — Gilbert Gurney 5101
—— — Widow and the Marquess, The . . 5102
Hooker, R.—Works of 2693-4
Hope, T.—Anastasius 5123-4
Hopkins, S.—Puritans, The 2660-1
—— — Youth of the Old Dominion . 3764
Horace—Works of 4197
Hornby, Mrs. E.—In and Around Stamboul . 1756
Hoskins, T. H.—What we Eat 2608
Houdin, R.—Memoirs of 1240
Hough, F. B.—Census of N. Y., 1855 . . 7694
Houssaye, A.—Men and Women of the xviii. Century 1001-2
—— — Philosophers and Actresses . 1003-4
Howard, W. A., et al.—Report of Com. on the Troubles in Kansas, 1856 . . 8614
Howe, Mrs. J. W.—Trip to Cuba, A . . 1905
—— W. W.—Pasha Papers, The . . . 3202
Howitt, W.—Homes and Haunts of the Poets . 3167-8
—— — Land, Labor and Gold . . . 1800-1
—— — Rural Life in England . . 3894-5
—— — Student Life in Germany . . 1562
—— — Visits to Remarkable Places . 1559-60
Huc, M.—Journey Through the Chinese Empire 1787-8
—— — Recollections of Tartary, Thibet, &c. 1793-4
Hudson, H. N.—Lectures on Shakspeare . . 3170-1
Hughes, T.—School Days at Rugby . . 5078
—— — Scouring the White Horse . . 5074
—— — Tom Brown at Oxford, vol. i., (2 copies) 5075-6
—— — " " " " " ii. . 5077
Hugo, V.—Rhine, The 1695

Knight, C. (Ed'r)—English Cyclopædia—Biography . 7812–14
——— — ——— " " Geography 7818–20
——— — ——— " " Nat. History 7824–7
——— — ——— Half-Hours with the Best Authors 3436–9
Knowles, J. S.—Dramatic Works of 4443–4
Kohl, J. G.—Russia 1565
Kohlrausch, F.—History of Germany 205
La Fontaine, J.—Fables 4241
Lamartine, A. de—History of the French Revolution of '48 511
——— ——— History of the Girondists . . . 995–7
——— ——— History of Turkey 621–3
——— ——— Memoirs of Celebrated Characters 998–1000
——— ——— Pilgrimage to the Holy Land . 1762–3
Lamb, C.—Specimens of Dramatic Poets 4449
——— — Works of 3422–3
Lander R. and J.—Journal of an Expedition to the Niger 1953–4
Landon, L. E. (Mrs. Maclean)—Complete Works of . 3511
Landor, W. S.—Pericles and Aspasia 3569–70
——— ——— Selections from 3330
——— ——— Works of 3514–15
Lane, E. W. (Ed'r)—Thousand-and-One Nights, The . 5210–12
Langdon, Mary—Agnes 5229
Lankester, (Dr.)—Vegetable Substances 2617
Lanman, C.—Summer in the Wilderness 1845
——— J. H.—History of Michigan 751
Lanzi, Luigi—History of Painting 3589–91
Lapham, I. A.—Antiquities of Wisconsin 7709
——— ——— Geographical and Typographical Description of Wisconsin 583
——— ——— Wisconsin 582
Lardner, D.—Popular Lectures on Science and Art . . 2292–3
Las Cases, Count de—Journal of Conversations with Napoleon 1222–5
Latrobe, C. J.—Rambler in Mexico 1867
Laurence, (?)—Sword and Gown 5235
——— R. (Trans'r)—Book of Enoch 2682
Lawrence, A.—Extracts from the Diary and Correspondence of 1343
Layard, A. H.—Discoveries in Nineveh and Babylon . 1496

Lewes, G. H.—Life and Works of J. W. von Goethe 1270-1

—— —— Life of M. Robespierre . . 1234

—— —— Physiology of Common Life . . 2359-60

Lewis, M. G.—Life and Carrespondence of . . 836-7

—— Lady T.—Semi-Detached House . . . 5226

Liebig, Baron von—Letters on Agriculture . . 2507

Lieber, F.—Civil Liberty and Self-Government . 2244-5

—— —— Essays on Property and Labor . . 2234

—— —— (Ed'r)—Encyclopædia Americana . . 7842-55

Liddell, H. G., and Scott, R.—Greek-English Lexicon 7891

Lincoln, A., and Douglas, S. A.—Political Debates between 2048

Lindsay, W. M.—Poems 4239

Lingard, J.—History of England . . . 82-9

Lipincott, Mrs. S. J. (Grace Greenwood)—Bonnie Scotland 5213

Lister, T. H.—Life of the Earl of Clarendon . . 813-15

Littell, E. (Ed'r)—Living Age, vols. i.-ix. . . 6959-67

—— —— " " vols. xx.-xxxi. . . 6979-90

—— —— " " vols. xl.-lxx. . 6999-7029

Livingstone, D.—Missionary Travels in Africa . . 1515

Livy, T.—History of Rome 415-18

Locke, J.—Conduct of the Understanding . . . 3078

Lockhart, J. G.—History of Bonaparte . . 1463-4

—— —— Memoirs of Sir W. Scott . . . 1174-80

—— —— (Trans'r)—Ancient Spanish Ballads . 4240

Longfellow, H. W.—Courtship of Miles Standish . . 4244

—— —— Golden Legend . . . 4245

—— —— Hyperien 5219

—— —— Kavanagh 5220

—— —— Outre Mer 1649

—— —— Poems 4242-3

—— —— Song of Hiawatha 4246

Loomis, E.—Introduction to Astronomy . . 2323

—— —— Recent Progress in Astronomy . . 2407

Loring, J. S.—Hundred Boston Orators, The . 2086

Lossing, B. J.—Biographical Sketches of the Signers 1039

—— —— Life and Times of P. Schuyler (vol. i.) 1322

—— —— Outline History of the Fine Arts . 3715

—— —— Pictorial Field Book 339-40

Loudon, Mrs. J. W.—Gardening for Ladies . . 2506

Lover, S.—Rory O'More, Handy Andy, &c. . 5894
———— — Songs and Ballads 4235
Lowell —New Priest of Conception Bay . 5200-1
——— J. R., (Homer Wilbur)—Biglow Papers . 3353
——— ——— Fable for Critics, A . . 4238
——— ——— Poems 4236-7
Lucian,—Comedies 4194
Lyell, Sir C.—Manual of Geology . . . 2307
——— ——— Second Visit to the U. S. . . 1833-4
——— ——— Travels in North America . . 1832
Lyman, S. P.—Public and Private Life of Webster 1332
Lynch, W. F.—Narrative of the Dead Sea Expedition 1497
Macaulay, L'd—Critical and Miscellaneous Essays . 3408-14
———— ——— History of England . . 466-70
———— ——— " " " vol. v. (Duplicate) 471
———— ——— Lays of Ancient Rome, &c. . 4258
———— ——— Speeches 5936-7
———— Miss—Tales of the Drama . . 5281
M'Clintock, Sir F. L.—Narrative of the Search for Sir J. Franklin . . . 1940
M'Cullock, J. R —Dictionary of Commerce . 7884-5
———— ——— Universal Gazetteer . . . 7906-7
Macfarlane, C.—Romance of History—Italy . 5301-2
Macgillivray, W.—Travels and Researches of Humboldt 1951
McHarg, C. K.—Life of Prince Talleyrand . . 1244
Machiavelli, N.—History of Florence . . 531
Macilwain, G.—Memoirs of J. Abernethy . . 1133
McIntosh, Maria J.—Meta Gray . . . 5285
———— ——— Two Lives 5286
Mackay, C.—Life and Liberty in America . . 1830-1
———— et al., (Ed'rs)—Illustrated London News, vols. xviii.-xxxviii. . 7945-65
Mackenzie, A. S.—Life of Paul Jones . . 1319-20
———— ——— Life of O. Perry . . . 1477-8
———— ——— Year in Spain, A . . 1712-14
———— H.—Miscellaneous Works of . . 3320
———— R. S.—Bits of Blarney . . . 3644
Mackey, A. G.—Lexicon of Free-Masonry . . 3059
Mackie, J. M.—Cosas de Espana . . . 1711

Marryat, F.—Jacob Faithful 4619
———— King's Own 4620
———— Masterman Ready 4545
———— Mr. Midshipman Easy . . . 4621
Marsh, Mrs.—History of the Reformation in France 2780-1
—— G. P.—Camel, The 2366
—— —— Lectures on the English Language 3748
Marshall, J.—Life of Geo. Washington . . 893-4
Martineau, J.—Endeavors after the Christian Life 2903
Marvell, A —Poetical Works of 4267
Mas, Poco—Scenes in Spain 1715
Massey, G.—Poems 4385
Massinger, P.—Plays of 4404
Masson, D.—British Novelists 3164
—— — Life of Milton 1441
Mather, C.—Magnalia Christi Americana . . 2658-9
—— W. W.—Annual Report of the Geol. Sur. of Ohio 2304
—— ——et al.—Rep. of the Geol. Sur. of N. Y. 1838-40 8842-3
Mathews, Mrs.—Memoirs of Chas. Mathews . 832-5
Maurice, F. D.—Religions of the World . . 2822
Maury, J. S.—Principles of Eloquence . . 3081
Maury, M. F.—Astronomical Observations, vol. v. 7415
—— —— Physical Geography of the Sea . 2291
Maxwell, W. H.—Fortunes of Hector O'Halloran 5283
May, Caroline, (Ed'r)—American Female Poets 4058
Mayer, B.—Mexico 322-3
Mayhew, H.—London Labor and London Poor, vols i.-iii. 2200-2
———— J. Popular Education 3799
Mayo, W. S.—Berber, The 5292
—— —— Kaloolah 3249
—— —— Romance Dust 5293
Mead, P. B.—Hay-time to Hopping . . 5306
—— —— Our Farm of Four Acres . . 2510
Meade, G. G.—Rep. on the Sur. of the N. and N. W. Lakes, '60 8667
Melville, G. J. W.—Holmby House 5896
———— H.—Confidence Man, The . . . 5260
———— — Israel Potter 5261
———— — Mardi 5262-3
———— — Moby Dick 5264
———— — Omoo 1922

Owen, D. D.—Report of a Geological Survey of Wisconsin, Iowa and Minnesota . 7456
—— R. D.—Footfalls on the Boundary of Another World 3046
Page, D. P.—Theory and Practice of Teaching . . 3798
—— T. J.—La Plata, &c. 1531
—— W. P.—Life and Writings of S. Johnson . . 1442–3
Paine, T.—Age of Reason 3036
—— — Poetical Works of 2243
Paley, F. A.—Manual of Gothic Architecture . 2534
—— W.—Natural Theology 2848
—— — Natural Theology (H. F. L.) . . 2944–5
—— — Works of 3087–91
Palfrey, J. G.—History of New England, vols. i.–ii. 267–8
Palmer, J. W.—Golden Dagon 1791
—— —— New and the Old, The . . . 1851
—— W.—Compendious Ecclesiastical History . 2767
Pardoe, Miss—Episodes in French History . . 504
—— —— Life Struggle, A 5343
—— —— Louis XIV. and the Court of France 513–14
Paris, J. A.—Philosophy in Sport 2396
Park, E. A., and Taylor, S. H. (Ed'rs)—Bibliothica Sacra, vol. xviii. 7345
Parker, E. G.—Reminiscences of R. Choate . 1339
—— H. F.—Discoverers and Pioneers of America 1843
—— N. H.—Iowa As It Is 580
—— S.—Journal of a Tour 1854
—— T.—Additional Speeches, Addresses, &c. . 2907–8
—— — Critical and Miscellaneous Writings . 3321
—— — Discourse of Religion 2909
—— — Experiences of a Minister . . . 1394
—— — Sermons on Theism, &c. . . . 2911
—— — Speeches, Addresses, &c. 2904–6
—— — Ten Sermons of Religion . . . 2910
Parkman, F., Jr.—History of the Conspiracy of Pontiac 353
Parkyns, M.—Abyssinia 1803–4
Parnell, T.—Poetical Works of 4298
Parrott, F —Journey to Ararat 1767
Parry, Sir W. E.—Three Voyages for the Discovery of a N. W. Passage . . 1958–9

Procter, B. W., (Barry Cornwall)—Dramatic Scenes, &c. 4450
—— —— English Songs, &c. 4291
—— —— Essays and Tales . . . 3342-3
—— —— Life of E. Kean 1152
Prout, W.—Chemistry, Meteorology and Digestion,—
(Br. Trea.) 2857
Pulszky, Theresa—Tales of Hungary 5342
Putnam, G. P., (Ed'r)—Hand B'k of Chronology and Hist. 7918
Pycroft, J.—Course of Reading 4002
Quin, M. J.—Steam Voyage down the Danube . 1696
Quincy, J.—Municipal History of Boston, . . 354
Uhden, H. F.—New England Theocracy . . 2792
Uhland, L., et al.—Songs and Ballads . . . 4341
Upham, C. W.—Life of J. C. Fremont . . 1338
—— T. C.—Life of M'me Guyon . . . 1245-6
—— —— Outlines of Disordered Mental Action 2616
Ure, A.—Dictionary of Arts, Manufactures and Mines 7882-3
Rabelais, F.—Works of 3444-5
Radcliffe, Mrs. A.—Mysteries of Udolpho, The . . 5379
—— —— Romance of the Forest, The . 5378
—— J. N.—Fiends, Ghosts and Sprites . . 3062
Ramsay, A., et al.—Gentle Shepherd, &c. . 4452
—— E. B.—Reminiscences of Scottish Life . 3669, 73
Randall, H. S.—Life of Jefferson . . . 898-900
Ranke, L.—History of the Popes 2677
Reade, C.—Christie Johnstone (2 copies) . . . 5394-5
—— — Clouds and Sunshine, &c. (2 copies) . 5396-7
—— — Eighth Commandment . . . 3041
—— — Good Fight, A, &c., ... 5398
—— — It is Never too Late to Mend, (2 copies) 5399-5402
—— — Love Me Little, Love Me Long, (2 copies) 5403-4
—— — Peg Woffington, (2 copies) . . 5405-6
—— — White Lies, (2 copies) . . . 5407-8
Read, T. B.—House by the Sea 4312
—— —— Sylvia, &c 4313
Redpath, J.—Public Life of John Brown, The . 1342
Reed, H.—Lectures on the British Poets . . . 3120-1
—— W. B.—Life and Correspondence of J. Reed . 908-9
—— —— et al.—Correspondence of Ministers to China 8668

Reid, M.—Boy Hunters, The 4547
—— — Boy Tar, The 4546
—— — Bruin (2 copies) 4548-9
—— — Bush Boys, The (2 copies) . . 4550-1
—— — Desert Home 4556
—— — Forest Exiles, The 4552
—— — Hunter's Feast, The 5386
—— — Odd People (2 copies) 2369-70
—— — Osceola 5387
—— — Plant Hunters, The (2 copies) . 4553, 7
—— — Quadroon 5388
—— — Ran away to Sea 4554
—— — Rifle Rangers, The 5389
—— — Scalp Hunters, The 5390
—— — War-Trail, The 5393
—— — White Chief, The 5392
—— — Wild Life 5391
—— — Young Voyageurs 4558
—— — Young Yagers 4555
Rennie, J.—Natural History of Birds . . . 2453
—— — Natural History of Insects . . 2451-2
—— — Natural History of Quadrupeds . 2459
—— — Natural History of the Elephant . 2454
Renwick, J.—Application of Mechanics to Practice 2554
—— — Life of De W. Clinton . . . 1479
—— — Lives of Jay and Hamilton . . 1427
Revere, J. W.—Tour in California . . . 1859
Reynold, J. N.—Pacific and Indian Oceans . 1491
Richardson, N. S., (Ed'r)—Am. Q. Church Review, vol. xiv. 7357
Richmond, J. C.—Metacomet 4314
—— — Midsummer's Day-Dream . 3711
Richter, J. P. F.—Life of 1272
Ripley, G., and Dana, C. A., (Ed'rs)—New American Cyclopædia, vols. i.-xi. 7791-7801
—— — — Taylor, B., (Ed'rs)—Hand Book of Literature and the Fine Arts 7920
Ritchie, Mrs. A. C., (Mowatt)—Autobiography of an Actress 1169
—— —— Mimic Life 5380
—— —— Plays 4451

Scott, Sir W.—Bride of Lammermoor, The, &c. (2 copies) 5468-9
—— —— Castle Dangerous and Tales of a Grandfather (2 copies) . . . 5496-5503
—— —— Chronicles of the Canongate (2 copies) 5472, 5504
—— —— Count Robert of Paris (2 copies) . 5470-1
—— —— Fortunes of Nigel, The (2 copies) . 5473-4
—— —— Guy Mannering (2 copies) . . 5475-6
—— —— Heart of Mid-Lothian, The (2 copies) . 5457-8
—— —— History of Scotland . . . 675-6
—— —— Ivanhoe 5479
—— —— Kenilworth (2 copies) . . . 5480-1
—— —— Letters on Demonology 3074
—— —— Letters on Magic 3075
—— —— Monastery, The (2 copies) . . 5482-3
—— —— Peveril of the Peak (2 copies) . . 5486-7
—— —— Pirate, The (2 copies) . . . 5484-5
—— —— Poetical Works of 4366-75
—— —— Quentin Durward (2 copies) . . 5488-9
—— —— Red Gauntlet 5490
—— —— Rob Roy 5491
—— —— St. Ronan's Well (2 copies) . . 5492-3
—— —— St. Valentine's Day (2 copies) . . 5494-5
—— —— Waverley 5505
—— —— Woodstock (2 copies) 5506-7
Sealsfield, C.—Cabin Book, The 3667
Seaman, E. C.—Essays on the Progress of Nations . 2197
Sedgwick, Mrs.—Alida 5556
—— Miss C. M.—Hope Leslie 5543-4
—— —— Letters from Abroad . . 1635-6
—— —— Linwoods, The . . . 5545-6
—— —— Redwood 5547
Segur, P. de—History of the Expedition to Russia . 681-2
Seneca, L. A.—Morals, by way of Abstract . . 3079
Sevigne, M'me de—Letters of 3852
Seward, W. H.—Life of J. Q. Adams . . . 1330
—— —— Works of 2199-11
Sewell, Miss—Amy Herbert 5557
—— —— Margaret Percival 5558-9
Seymour, C. C. B.—Self-Made Men 1036

Stone, W. L.—Border Wars 748-9
—— —— Life of J. Brant . . 920-1
Story, J.—Commentaries on the Constitution . 2171
—— — Life and Letters of 913-14
—— — Miscellaneous Writings of . . , 3539
Storrs, R. S., Jr.—Constitution of the Soul . 2963
Stowe, Mrs. H. B.—Dred 5508-9
—— —— Minister's Wooing, The (2 copies) 5510 11
—— —— Sunny Memories . . . 1646-7
—— —— Uncle Tom's Cabin . . 5512-13
Strauss, D. F.—Life of Jesus 2959-60
Street, A. B.—Woods and Waters . . . 3898
Strickland, Miss A.—Lives of the Queens of England 778-83
—— —— Lives of the Queens of Scotland 961-8
—— W. P.—Old Mackinaw 5561
Stuart, J., and Revett, N.—Antiquities of Athens . 409
Stuart, R.—Cyclopedia of Architecture . . . 2531
Sturn, C. C.—Reflections 2863-4
Sue, E.—Mysteries of Paris 5900
—— — Price of a Crown 5563
—— — Wandering Jew, The 5899
Sullivan, W.—Public Men of the Revolution . . 800
Sully, Duke of—Memoirs of 515-19
Sumner, C.—Orations and Speeches . . . 3933-4
—— — Recent Speeches and Addresses . . 3935
Surry, Earl of, (H. Howard)—Poetical Works of . 4339
Sutherland, A.—Achievements of the Knights of Malta 433
Swedenborg, E.—Angelic Wisdom Concerning Divine Love 2751
—— — " " " " Providence 2752
—— — Apocalypse Explained . . 2743-7
—— — " Revealed . . . 2748-9
—— — Arcana Cœlestia 2733-42
—— — Conjugial Love 2750
—— — Four Leading Doctrines . . 2753
—— — Heaven and Hell 2754
—— — Miscellaneous Theological Works 2755
—— — True Christian Religion . . 2756
Swift, J.—Gulliver's Travels 5562
—— — Poetical Works of 4315-17
—— — Works of 3402-7

Taylor, Z., et al.—Mess. of the Pres. of the U. S. and Accompanying Documents, 1851–4 8162-8

—— —— " " " " 1855–60 8173-91

Temple, F., et al.—Recent Inquiries in Theology,—("Essays and Reviews") . . 2851

Tennent, J. E.—Belgium 1693-4

Tennyson, A.—Idyls of the King . . . - . 4326

—— — Poems 4324-5

Tensas, M.—Odd Leaves from the Note Book of a Swamp Doctor 3234

Thacher, J.—Military Journal of the Revolution . 342

Thackeray, W. M.—Ballads 4327

—— —— Book of Snobs, and Yellowplush Papers 5623

—— —— English Humorists . . 3144

—— —— Four Georges, The . . . 3143

—— —— History of Henry Esmond . 5841

—— —— History of Henry Esmond, &c. . 5842

—— —— History of Pendennis (2 copies) 5846-9

—— —— Jeames' Diary, and Fitz Boodle . 6624

—— —— Lovel the Widower (2 copies) 5843-4

—— —— Luck of Barry Lyndon . . 5625

—— —— Men's Wives, and Shabby Genteel Story 5626

—— —— Mr. Brown's Letters . . 3207

—— —— Mr. Brown's Letters, and Punch's Novelists 5627

—— —— Newcomes, The . . . 5845

—— —— Notes of a Journey to Grand Cairo 1813

—— —— Rose and the Ring, The . . 5628

—— —— Paris Sketch Book . . 1687

—— —— Vanity Fair (2 copies) . . 5851-2

—— —— Virginians, The . . . 5850

—— —— (Ed'r)—Cornhill Magazine, The vols. i.–iii. . . 6035-7

Thatcher, B. B.—Indian Biography 1428-9

Thierry, A.—History of the Conquest of England . 473-4

Thiers, L. A.—French Revolution 158-9

—— —— History of the Consulate and Empire 160-2

Thirlwall, C.—History of Greece 33-4

N

CATALOGUE

OF THE LIBRARY OF THE

Young Men's Association

OF THE

CITY OF MILWAUKEE.

PART II.—BY TITLES.

Title	Author	No.
Abbot, The, (2 copies)	*Scott*	5459–60
Abridgment of the Debates of Congress .	*Benton*	1976–91
Acadia	*Cozzens*	1914
Accompaniment to Map of the World .	*Mitchell*	6
Account of Expeditions to the Mississippi .	*Pike*	1521
Achievements of the Knights of Malta	*Sutherland*	433
Adam Bede	*Miss Evans*	4989
Adaptation of External Nature (Br. Trea.)	*Chalmers*	2853
" " " " "	*Kidd*	2854
Additional Speeches, Addresses, &c. .	*Parker*	2907–8
Adirondack, The	*Headley*	3893
Adolphe Renouard	*Ward*	5696
Adventures and Observations in Africa .	*Thomas*	1814
" in Africa	*Harris*	1511
" of Capt. Bonneville . .	*Irving*	1863
" " *Gerard* (The Lion Killer)		1819
" " Gil Blas	*Le Sage*	5207–9
" " Mr. Ledbury and his Friend	*Smith*	5567
" " Telemachus	*Fenelon*	4605
" " Verdant Green . . .	*Bede*	4697

Title	Author	No.
Annals of San Francisco . .	*Soule, et al.*	355
" " the American Pulpit .	*Sprague*	2702--8
" " Queens of Spain	*Anita George*	1017--18
Anne of Geierstein . . .	*Scott*	5461
Annual of Scientific Discovery, 1850-61	*Wells*	2417--28
" Rep. of the Com. of Patents, 1847-8	*Burke, et al.*	8102--4
" " " " " 1849–51, Agri.	"	8105–7
" " " " " 1854-9	" "	8108–113
" " " " " 1849, 1851-9 Mech.	"	8114–32
" " of the Geol. Surv. of Ohio .	*Mather*	2304
" " " Smithsonian Instit'n, 1853-7	*Henry, et al.*	8624–8
" State. of the T. and Com. of Milwaukee,	*Crounse*	2214
Antiquary, The (2 copies) . . .	*Scott*	5462–3
Antiquities of Athens .	*Stewart and Revett*	409
" of Wisconsin . . .	*Lapham*	7709
Apocalypse Explained . . .	*Swedenborg*	2743–7
" Revealed . .	"	2748–9
Apochryphal New Testament		2865
Appleton's Dictionary of Machines, Mechanics, &c.		7888–9
" Library Manual, 1847		3998
" Mechanic's Mag., vol. i., edited by	*Adams*	5966
" Mech. Mag., vols. ii.–iii., "	"	7723–4
Applications of Mechanics to Practice .	*Renwick*	2554
Arabian Days, translated by *Curtis* . . .		4836
Arcana Cœlestia . . .	*Swendenborg*	2733–42
Architecture of Country Houses . .	*Downing*	2523
" of the Heavens . . .	*Nichol*	2321
Arctic Boat Journey	*Hayes*	1941
Arctic Explorations	*Kane*	1500–1
Artist-Life	*Tuckerman*	1073
Arthur Mervyn	*Brown*	4704–5
Art Journal, The, vol. xiii.		7716
Aspects of Nature	*Humboldt*	2351
Aspen Court	*Brooks*	4721
Assembly of Wis.—Trial of Impeachment, 1853 .		8833
Astoria	*Irving*	1853
Astronomical Observations, vol. v. .	*Maury*	7415
Astronomy and General Physics (Br. Trea.)	*Whewell*	2852
Athens	*Bulwer*	407–8

At Homeand Abro ad . *Countess D'Ossoli* 1628
" " . . . . . *Taylor* 1616
Atlantic Monthly, vols. i.–vii. 7244–50
Atlas of the World . . . . . *Colton* 7942–3
Attache, The . . . . . . *Haliburton* 1653
Attache in Madrid, The . . . *Goodrich* 1710
Attic Philosopher . . . . . *Souvestre* 3033
Attorney, The . . . . . . *Irving* 5145
Aubrey Conyers . . . . . *Miss Stewart* 5555
Audobon: his Adven. and Discoveries *Mrs. St. John* 1355
Aurelian . . . . *Ware* 4487–8
Aurora Leigh . . . . *Mrs. Browning* 4107
Australia . . . . . . *Pridden* 631
Australian Crusoes . . . . *Rowcroft* 5385
Autobiographic Sketches . . . *De Quincey* 1139
Autobiographical Recollections . . *Leslie* 1144
Autobiography of a Seaman . . *Dundonald* 844–5
" of an Actress . *Mrs. Ritchie* 1169
" of *A. Carlyle* 1173
" of *Mrs. Piozzi* (Thrale) . . 1165
Autocrat of the Breakfast-Table . . *Holmes* 3231
Avenger, The, &c. . . . . . *De Quincey* 3253
Ballad of Babie Bell, &c. . . . *Aldrich* 4085
Ballads . . . . *Homer* 4195
" . . . . *Thackeray* 4327
" of Scotland, edited by *Aytoun* 4081–2
Barnaby Rudge . . . . . *Dickens* 4910
Baths, and Watering Places . . . . . *Lee* 2610
Battle-Fields . . . . . . *Harrison* 341
Bay Path, The . . . . *Holland* 5103
Beatrice Cenci . . . . . *Guerrazzi* 5058
Beauchampe . . . . *Simms* 5514
Beaumarchais and his Times . . *De Lomenie* 1236
Beauties, Harmonies and Sublimities of Nature *Bucke* 2450
Belgium . . . . *Tennent* 1693–4
Berber, The . . . . *Mayo* 5292
Betrothed, The (I Promessi Spozi) . *Manzoni* 5280
" " and Talisman, The (2 copies) *Scott* 5464–5
Beulah (2 copies) . . . . . *Miss Evans* 4987–8

Title	Author	No.
Brambletye House	*Smith*	5570
Brandon	*Tiffany*	5653
Bravo, The (2 copies)	*Cooper*	4763–4
Brazil and the Brazilians	*Kidder and Fletcher*	1530
Bride of Lammermoor, &c. (2 copies)	*Scott*	5468–9
British Drama	*Garrick, et al.*	4416–17
British Expedition to the Crimea	*Russell*	387
British Manly Exercises	*Walker*	3838
British Novelists	*Masson*	3164
Bruin (2 copies)	*Reid*	4548–9
Bubbles frem the Brunnen	*Head*	1700
Buried Cities of the East—Nineveh		1775
Bush-Boys, The (2 copies)	*Reid*	4550–1
Cabin Boy, The	*Sealsfield*	3667
Cæsars, The	*De Quincey*	3115
Cakes and Ale	*Jerrold*	3646
Calamities of Authors	*D'Israeli*	3146
California: In-Doors and Out	*Mrs. Farnham*	1860
Callista	*Newman*	4492
Camel, The	*Marsh*	2366
Campaign Sketches	*Henry*	606
Canada, Nova Scotia, &c.	*Buckingham*	1507
Canterbury Tales	*Harriet Lee*	5197–8
" "	*Sophia Lee*	5199
Capt. Cook's Voyages	*Barrow*	1938
Captains of the Roman Republic	*Herbert*	3145
Careful Enquiry on Freedom of the Will	*Edwards*	2697
Carthage and Her Remains	*Davis*	1516
Castle Dangerous, and Tales of a Grandfather, (2 copies)	*Scott*	5496–5503
Catalogue of Books, 1831	*Bohn*	3999
" of the Lib. of the Hartford Y. M. Inst., '44		3997
" of the Mercantile Library in N. Y., '37, '50		3995–6
" " N. Y. State Library, 1850		3985
" " " " 1855—General		3986
" " " " 1855—Law		3987
" " " " 1856—Maps, &c.		3988
" " " " 1858—Bibliography		3989
" " " Trade Sale, 1853		4000

Critical and Miscellaneous Writings .	*Talfourd*	3547
" Dict. of Eng. Literature, vol. i.	*Allibone*	7868
Critique of Pure Reason	*Kant*	3024
Crock of Gold, The	*Tupper*	5651
Crossed Path, The	*Collins*	4846
Cruise of the Midge . .	*M. Scott* (?)	5818
" " North Star . . .	*Choules*	1645
Curiosities of Literature . .	*D'Israeli*	3427-30
" " Natural History . .	*Buckland*	2364-5
Currents and Counter-Currents . .	*Holmes*	3319
Cyril Thornton	*Hamilton*	5112
Cyclopædia of Am. Liter., edited by *Bro's*	*Duyckinck*	7874-5
" " Architecture . .	*Stuart*	7923
" " Eng. Literature, edited by	*Chambers*	7870-1
" " Practical Receipts .	*Cooley*	7887
" " Wit and Humor . .	*Burton*	3582–3
Cyropædia	*Xenophon*	658
Dahcotah	*Mrs. Eastman*	4999
Daily Duties	*Mrs. Adams*	3863
Daltons, The (2 copies) . . .	*Lever*	5866–8
Daniel Boone and the Hunters of Ky.	*Bogart*	1328
Danish Story Book	*Andersen*	4611
Davenport Dunn (2 copies) . .	*Lever*	5864–5
David Copperfield (2 copies) . .	*Dickens*	4923–5
Days of Bruce, The . .	*Grace Aguilar*	4632–3
Day's Ride, A (2 copies) . .	*Lever*	5883–4
Dead Secret, The	*Collins*	4848
Dealings with the Dead	*Sargent*	3567–8
Dear Experience	*Ruffini*	5368
Decameron, The , ...	*Boccaccio*	3233
Deck and Port	*Colton*	1862
Deer Slayer, The (2 copies) .	*Cooper*	4769–71
Democracy	*Camp*	2235
" in America . . .	*De Tocqueville*	2028–9
Demonstration of the Truth of Christianity	*Keith*	2866
De Officiis, ...	*Cicero*	4022
Description of Pitcairn's Island . .	*Barrow*	754
Description of the Canals and R. R. of the U.S.	*Tanner*	2199
Des. and Hist. Acc't of Hydraulic Machines	*Ewbank*	2530

Title	Author	No.
Desert Home	*Reid*	4556
De Vere	*Ward*	5691–2
Devereaux	*Bulwer*	4660
Devil on Two Sticks, &c.	*LeSage*	3709
Diary and Correspondence of *S. Pepys* . .		105–8
" " Letters of *M'me D'Arblay* (Miss Burney)		1153–9
" A, H—— Family, &c. .	*Miss Bremer*	4689
" of an Ennuyee . . .	*Mrs. Jameson*	3723
" " the Times of Charles II. . .	*Sidney*	109–10
" " Washington		1314
Dictionary of Americanisms	*Bartlett*	7921
" " Antiquities, A, edited by *Smith* .		7896
" " Arts, Manufactures and Mines	*Ure*	7882–3
" " Commerce	*M'Culloch*	7884–5
" " Poetical Quotations, edited by *Watson*		7926
" " Science, Literature and Art	*Brande*	7895
" " the English Language .	*Johnson*	7890
Dies Boreales	*Wilson*	3377
Digest of the U. S. Laws	*Gordon*	2173
Diplomatic and Official Papers of *Webster* . .		2118
Discourse of Natural Theology . .	*Brougham*	2847
" " Religion	*Parker*	2909
" on the Adv. and Plea. of Science	*Brougham, et al.*	2325
Discourses, Charges, &c.	*Potter*	2899
" on Government	*Sidney*	2055–7
" " Science and Literature	*Brougham, et al.*	2468
Discoverers and Pioneers of America .	*Parker*	1843
Discoveries in Nineveh and Babylon .	*Layard*	1496
Discovery and Expl. of the Miss. Valley	*Shea*	311
Disowned, The	*Bulwer*	4661
Distinguished Men of Modern Times .	*Malden*	1433–4
Diversions of Purley	*Tooke*	3749
Doctor, The, &c.	*Southey*	3556
Doctor Antonio	*Ruffini*	5369
" Oldham at Grey Stones	*Henry*	3217
Documentary History of N. Y., edited by	*O'Callaghan*	7589–92
Doc'ts Relative to the Col. His. of N. Y. "	"	7725–34
Dog, The	*Youatt*	2482
Dombey and Son	*Dickens*	4915

Domestic History of the Revolution .	*Mrs. Ellet*	567
" Slavery, (a Correspondence)	*Fuller & Wayland*	3086
Don Quixote	*Cervantes*	5820–1
Dorothy		5728
Dramas, &c.	*Hillhouse*	4459–60
Dramas, vol. i.	*Byron*	4472
Dramatic Scenes, &c.	*Procter*	4450
Dramatic Works of *Farquhar G.* . . .		4402
" " of *Ford, J.*		4427–8
" " of *Goethe, J. W. von* . .		4439
" " of *Knowles, J. S.* . .		4443–4
" " of *Sheridan, R. B.* . .		4440
" " of *Vanbrugh, Sir. J.* . .		4402
" " of *Webster, J.* . . .		4455–8
" " of *Wycherley, W.* . .		4402
Dream Life	*Mitchell*	3236
Dred	*Mrs. Stowe*	5508–9
Dyer's Assistant	*Haigh*	2541
Early Jesuit Missions	*Kip*	2793
Earth, The	*Higgins*	2449
" and Man	*Guyot*	2383
Ecclesiastical History	*Moshiem*	2638
Eclipse of Faith	*Rogers*	2844
Edgar Huntley	*Brown*	4706
Edinburgh Jour., vols. xvii.-xx., edited by	*Bro. Chambers*	7109–11
" " vols. i.-xiv., N. S. "	"	7112–20
Edinburgh Review, The (odd nos.) . . .		7062–4
" " vols. lxxxvii.-xcii. . . .		7065–7
" " " xcv.-viii. . .		7069–70
" " " ci.-xii.		7072–7
Edith Allen	*Neville*	5328
Edith Hale	*Talmon*	5729
Education	*Smith*	3804
"	*Spencer*	3800
Eighth Commandment	*Reade*	3041
El Buscapie	*Cervantes*	3210
Eldorado	*Taylor*	1864
Elementary Treatise on Mineralogy .	*Phillips*	2310

English Woman in Russia		1745
Eothen	*Warburton*	1764
Epicurean, The	*Moore*	5282
Episodes in French History	*Miss Pardoe*	504
Epitome of the History of Philosophy	*Henry*	3076–7
Ernest Maltravers	*Bulwer*	4662–3
Essay on Universal History	*Voltaire*	403–6
" on Washington	*Guizot*	3126
Essays	*Bacon*	3078
"	*Emerson*	3344–5
"	*Foster*	3714
"	*Spencer*	3551
"	*Tuckerman*	3552
" and Advancement of Learning	*Bacon*	3329
" and Reviews	*Brownson*	3318
" "	*Whipple*	3161
" and Tales	*Procter*	3342–3
" in Biography and Criticism	*Bayne*	3151–2
" on Morality	*Dymond*	2975
" on Philosophical Writers	*De Quincey*	3118–19
" on Property and Labor	*Lieber*	2234
" on the Poets	*De Quincey*	3154
" on the Progress of Nations	*Seaman*	2197
" on Various Subjects	*Hume*	3549
Eugene Aram	*Bulwer*	4664
European Civilization	*Balmes*	2678
" Life and Manners	*Colman*	5517–18
Eutaw (2 copies)	*Simms*	1617–18
Euthanasy	*Mountford*	2914
Executive Doc'ts of the U. S. House of Rep.:		
1855-6, vols. ii., v., vii., ix., xi., xii., xv.		8427–33
1856-7, vols. v., vi., ix., x., xii.,		8434–8
1857-8, vols. iii., vii., ix., x., xii., xiii.,		8439–44
1858-9, vols. i., iii., v., vii., ix., xii.		8445–50
1859-60, vols. i., iv., v., vi., viii., ix., xii., xiii.		8451–8
Executive Doc'ts of the U. S. H. of Rep. on Central American Affairs	*Marcy, et al.*	8663
Executive Doc'ts of the U. S. H. of Rep. on the Mexican War	*Polk, et al.*	8660

Title	Author	No.
Executive Doc'ts of the U. S. Senate:		
1855-6, vols. vi., x., xii.-xvi.		8231–7
1856-7, vols., v.-viii.		8238–41
1757-8, vols., vi., xii., xiii.		8242–4
1858-9, vols. vi., (2 p'ts) vii., x.		8245–8
1859–60, vols. v., ix., xi.		8249–51
Rel. to Kansas, 1855-6	*Marcy, et al.*	8613
Exemplary Novels of *M. de Cervantes*		4831
Exiles of Florida	*Giddings*	3661
" " Siberia	*M'me Cottin*	5573
Expedition to Borneo	*Keppel*	1792
Experience as a Minister	*Parker*	1394
" of a Barrister	*Warren* (?)	5698
Exploration of the Amazon, with Maps	*Gibbon*	1528–9
" " " "	*Herndon*	1526–7
Explorations and Adventures in Africa	*Du Chaillu*	1513
Exploring Expedition to Oregon, &c.	*Fremont*	1856
Exposition of the xxxix. Articles	*Fowler*	2870
Extracts from the Diary and Corres. of	*A. Lawrence*	1343
Evelina	*M'me D'Arblay*	4899
Fabiola	*Wiseman*	4493
Fables	*Æsop*	3713
"	*La Fontaine*	4241
" for Critics	*Lowell*	4338
Facts and Speculations on the History of Cards	*Chatto*	3815
Faggot of French Sticks	*Head*	1683
Fairy Mythology	*Keightley*	3064
Faithful Forever	*Patmore*	4294
Family Encyclopædia	*Blake*	7886
Familiar Anecdotes of Sir W. Scott	*Hogg*	1181
" Introduction to Heraldry	*Barrington*	499
Famous Persons and Places	*Willis*	1655
Father and Daughter (2 copies)	*Miss Bremer*	4690–1
Faust	*Goethe*	4181
Federalist, The	*Hamilton, et al.*	2053
Fern Leaves	*Mrs. Parton*	3214
Festivals, Games and Amusements	*Smith*	3839
Festus	*Bailey*	4101
Few Days in Athens, A	*Frances Wright*	3666
Field Sports in the South	*Whitehead*	5694

Title	Author	No.
Game of Billiards, The	*Phelan*	3835
Gardening for Ladies . .	*Mrs. Loudon*	2506
Gazetteer of Massachusetts . .	*Spofford*	7928
" of New Hampshire	*Farmer and Moore*	7927
Geneological and Heraldic Dictionary . .	*Burke*	7877
" Dictionary of New England	*Savage*	7878–9
General Biographical Dictionary . .	*Gorton*	7913–15
" History of Civilization . .	*Guizot*	2257
" " of the Church . .	*Neander*	2642–5
" View of Christianity . .	*Whately*	2796
" " of the Fine Arts .	*Huntington*	3595
" " of the Prog. of Philosophy	*Mackintosh*	2974
Genesis and Geology	*Crofton*	2375
Genius of Burns	*Wilson*	3147
" of Christianity . .	*Chateaubriand*	2690
" of Scotland	*Turnbull*	3070
Gentle Shepherd, &c. . . .	*Ramsay, et al.*	4452
Geo. and Top. Description of Wisconsin	*Lapham*	583
Georgian Era		957–60
Gerald Fitzgerald	*Lever*	5869
German Literature	*Menzel*	3424–6
" Popular Tales . .	*Brothers Grimm*	5050–1
Germany	*Schaff*	2820
Gilbert Gurney	*Hook*	5101
Gipsy's Prophecy, The .	*Mrs. Southworth*	5574
Glances and Glimpses . .	*Harriot K. Hunt*	1348
Glaucus	*Kingsley*	3902
Gleanings	*Miss Goddard*	3196
Godolphin	*Bulwer*	4665
Golden Dagon	*Palmer*	1791
" Legend	*Longfellow*	4245
Gold Foil	*Holland*	3314
Good Fight, A, &c.	*Reade*	5398
Gospel in Ezekiel	*Guthrie*	2900
Grammar of Chemistry	*Comstock*	2400
" " the Latin Language	*Andrews and Stoddard*	4020
Grantley Manor	*Lady Fullerton*	5027
Great Expectations (2 copies) .	*Dickens*	5830–1
Greatness and Decline of Cesar Birotteau	*Balzac*	4724

Title	Author	No.
Greek-English Lexicon	*Liddell and Scott*	7891
Geen Mountain Boys	*Thompson*	5648
Greyson Letters	*Rogers*	1143
Guesses at Truth	*Brothers Hare*	3317
Gulliver's Travels	*Swift*	5562
Guy Mannering (2 copies)	*Scott*	5475–6
Guy Rivers (2 copies)	*Simms*	5521–2
Half-Hours with the Best Authors, edited by	*Knight*	3436–9
Hallig, The	*Biernatzki*	4480
Hallucinations	*Boismont*	2324
Hamiltons, The	*Mrs. Gore*	5063
Hand Book for Readers	*Potter*	4013
" " " Volunteers	*Viele*	2540
" " of Chronology and Hist., edited by	*Putnam*	7918
" " " Lit. and the Fine Arts "	*Ripley & Taylor*	7920
" " " Univ. Biography, edited by	*Godwin*	7916
" " " " Geography, edited by	*Callicot*	7917
" " " Useful Arts, edited by	*Antisell*	7919
" " " Wisconsin	*Chapman*	584
Handy Book on Property Law	*St. Leonards*	2267
Harold	*Bulwer*	4666
Harper's Magazine, vol. i.		7212
" " " iv.-xxii.		7215–33
" Weekly, 1859-60		7970–1
Harry Harson	*Irving*	5146
" Lorrequer, &c. (2 copies)	*Lever*	5870–1
Haunted House, The	*Dickens*	5829
Hay-time to Hopping	*Mead*	5306
Headsman, The (2 copies)	*Cooper*	4772–3
Health and Disease	*Hall*	2607
" Trip	*Willis*	1901
Heart of Mid-Lothian, (2 copies)	*Scott*	5477–8
" " Mabel Ware		5731
Heaven and Hell	*Swedenborg*	2754
Heidenmauer, (2 copies)	*Cooper*	4774–5
Heiress of Brugess, The	*Grattan*	5060
Heir of Redcliffe, The	*Miss Yonge*	5701–2
Henrietta Temple	*D'Israeli*	4932
Heptameron, The	*Margaret of Navarre*	4307

Hermann and Dorothea . . . *Goethe* 4182
Heroes, Hero-Worship, &c . . *Carlyle* 3125
Hesperian, The, vol. ii., edited by *Gallagher* . 5965
Hesperides, &c. . . . . . *Herrick* 4205–6
Hide and Seek . . . . . *Collins* 5802
Hills, Lakes and Forest Streams . *Hammond* 1850
Hints on Angling . . . . . *Hackle* 3816
" " Public Architecture . . *Owen* 7708
Histriarum Libri Quinque . . *Tacitus* 4021
Hist. Acc't of the Circumnavigation of the Globe 1945
Historical and Critical Essays . *De Quincey* 3671–2
" " " View of Philosophy *Morrell* 2954
" " Des. Acc't of B. America . *Murray* 715–16
" " " " " " India *Murray, et al.* 729–31
" " " " " Iceland, &c. . *Nicol* 708
" " " " " Persia . *Fraser* 738
" " Sec. Mem. of Josephine *M'me LeNormand* 1229–30
Historical Memoirs . . . . . *Wraxall* 115
" Sketch of the 2d War . *Ingersoll* 343
" Sketches of Statesmen . *Brougham* 949–50
" Studies . . . . . *Greene* 3141
" View of the Dis. of America *Tytler* 1947
" View of the Lang. and Lit. of the Slavic Nations *Mrs. Robinson* 3663
" View of the Lit. of the S. of Europe *Sismondi* 3309–10
Historic Doubts relative to Napoleon . *Whately* 3029
History . . . . *Heroditus* 410
" Habits and Ins'ts of Animals (Br. Trea.) *Kirby* 2855–6
" of America . . . . . *Robertson* 218
" " (abridged) . . . . " 714
" American Privateers . . *Coggeshall* 346
" an Adopted Child . . *Miss Jewsbury* 5174
" Arabia . . . . . *Crichton* 736–7
" Architecture . . . *Mrs. Tuthill* 2524
" Bonaparte . . . . *Abbott* 873–4
" " . . . . *Lockhart* 1463–4
" Charles XII. . . . . . *Voltaire* 1470
" Chivalry . . . . . . *James* 713
" Civilization . . . *Guizot* 2250–2

History of Civilization in England .	*Buckle*	2025–6
" Connecticut	*Dwight*	750
" Cromwell, &c. . . .	*Guizot*	1106–7
" England	*Hume*	73–6
" "	*Keightly*	660–4
" "	*Lingard*	82–9
" "	*Macaulay*	466–70
" " vol. v. (duplicate) .	"	471
" "	*Mackintosh*	965–7
" "	*Mahon*	90–6
" "	*Smollett*	77–8
" Europe, '89–'15 . . .	*Alison*	60–3
" " '15–'52 . . .	"	64–72
" Fiction	*Dunlop*	3508
" Florence	*Machiavelli*	531
" France	*Crowe*	677–9
" " (vol. i.) . . .	*Godwin*	151
" "	*Michelet*	155–6
" Frederick II., vols. i.-ii. .	*Carlyle*	1278–9
" Germany . . .	*Kohlrausch*	205
" Greece	*Mitford*	25–32
" "	*Thirlwall*	33–4
" Henry Esmond (2 copies) .	*Thackeray*	5841–2
" Inventions . . .	*Beckmann*	2414–15
" Ireland	*Moore*	144–5
" "	*Taylor*	673–4
" Latin Christianity . . .	*Milman*	2768–72
" Lewis and Clarke's Expedition	*Allen*	1961–2
" Liberty—Ancient Romans .	*Eliot*	2049–50
" " Early Christians .	"	2051–2
" Louisiana	*Bunner*	752
" "	*Gayarre*	310
" Magic . . .	*Ennemoser*	3060–1
" Massachusetts .	*Bradford*	308
" " . . .	*Hutchinson*	568–71
" Michigan	*Lanman*	751
" New England (vols. i.-ii.) .	*Palfrey*	267–8
" " " . . .	*Winthrop*	275–6
" New Netherland . .	*O'Callaghan*	291–2

Title	Author	No.
History of the English Reformation . .	*Burnet*	2648–50
" " " " .	*Cobbett*	2782
" " " Revolution . .	*Guizot*	475
" " Expedition to Russia .	*Segur*	681–2
" " Four Georges . , .	*Smucker*	955
" " French Protestant Refugees	*Weiss*	2789–90
" " " Revolution (vol. i.)	*Blanc*	165
" " French Revolution .	*Mignet*	509
" " " " of '48	*Lamartine*	511
" " Girondists . . .	"	995–7
" " Hartford Convention . .	*Dwight*	2054
" " House of Austria . . .	*Coxe*	543–5
" " Inductive Sciences . .	*Whewell*	2294–5
" " Insurrection in China	*Callery & Yvan*	628
" " Italian Republics . .	*Sismondi*	696
" " Jesuits . . .	*Steinmetz*	2679–81
" " Jews	*Milman*	648–50
" " Later Roman Commonwealth	*Arnold*	41
" " Life of Loyola, . . .	*Bartoli*	1387–8
" " " Madison, vol. i.	*Rives*	903
" " Martyrs	*Fox*	2795
" " Mississippi Valley . .	*Monette*	312–13
" " Moors of Spain . .	*Florian*	711
" " Netherlands . . .	*Grattan*	688
" " Order of St. John of Jerusalem	*Taffe*	52–3
" " Peloponnesian War .	*Thucydides*	411–12
" " Peninsular War . . .	*Napier*	533–7
" " Popes	*Ranke*	2677
" " Protest. Church in Hungary	*D'Aubigne*	2788
" " Puritans	*Neal*	2663–4
" " Reformation . .	*D'Aubigne*	2776–9
" " "	*Spalding*	2651–2
" " " in France	*Mrs. Marsh*	2780–1
" " Reign of Charles V. .	*Robertson*	206
" " " " (abridged)	"	683
" " " Ferdinand and Isabella	*Prescott*	215–17
" " " George III. . .	*Bissett*	212–14
" " " Philip II. . .	*Prescott*	212–14

Title	Author	No.
Hours with My Pupils	*Mrs. Phelps*	3854
House by the Sea	*Read*	4312
Household Book of Poetry, edited by *Dana*		4033
" of Bouverie	*Mrs. Warfield*	5699–5700
House of Seven Gables, The	*Hawthorne*	5082
" on the Moor, The	*Mrs. Oliphant*	5331
Howadji in Syria	*Curtis*	1765
How I Tamed Mrs. Cruiser	*Sala*	3198
Hudibras	*Butler*	4111
Huguenot Exiles		5730
Human Body, The	*Wilkinson*	3030
" Health	*Dunglison*	2593
Humorous Poetry, edited by *Parton*		4287
" Stories	*Brougham*	4698
Humors of Falconbridge	*Kelley*	3634
Hundred Boston Orators, The	*Loring*	2086
Hungary in '51	*Brace*	1699
Hunter's Feast, The	*Reid*	5386
Hurry-Graphs	*Willis*	3221
Hypatia	*Kingsley*	4485–6
Hyperian	*Longfellow*	5219
Iconographic Encyclopædia, edited by *Heck*		7862–5
" " plates, "		7866–7
Idyls of the King	*Tennyson*	4326
Iliad, The	*Homer*	4196
Illustrated London News, vols. xviii.–xxxviii., edited by	*Mackay, et al.*	7945–65
Illustrations of Genius	*Giles*	3149
" of Mechanics	*Moseley*	2469
" of North American Birds	*Cassin*	2313
" of the Man'rs, &c., of the N. A. Indians—	*Catlin*	349–50
Imitation of Christ	*Kempis*	2861
Impending Crisis, The	*Helper*	2255
Importance of Education	*Everett*	3801
Improvement of Society	*Dick*	3085
In and Around Stamboul	*Hornby*	1756
Incidents of American History	*Barber*	568

Incidents of Travel in Egypt, &c. .	*Stephens*	1810–11
" of Travel in Greece, &c. .	"	1630–1
" " Yucatan . .	"	1599–1600
Index to Periodical Literature . .	*Poole*	3991
India	*Allen*	384
" and the Hindoos	*Ward*	525
Indian Biography	*Thatcher*	1428–9
" Wars of the U. S.	*Frost*	352
" " " "	*Moore*	351
Infantry Tactics	*Scott*	2555–7
Information for the People, edited by *Bro's*	*Chambers*	7872–3
Ingenue	*Dumas*	4901
Ingoldsby Legends	*Barham*	4702–3
Initials, The . .	*Baroness Tautphœus*	5634
Inquiries Concerning the Intel. Powers	*Abercrombie*	3083
Inquiry into the Wealth of Nations . .	*Smith*	2195
Ins and Outs of Paris . .	*M'me Marguerittes*	1685
Instruction for Field Artillery .	*French, et al.*	2543
Instructions to Young Sportsmen . .	*Hawker*	3819
International Magazine, vols. ii.-iv. . . .		5962–4
Introduction to Astronomy	*Loomis*	2323
" "	*Olmsted*	2322
" Geology	*Bakewell*	2306
" International Law .	*Woolsey*	2263
" the Literature of Europe	*Hallam*	3504–5
Introductory Lectures on Modern History	*Arnold*	438
" Lessons on Mind . .	*Whately*	3026
Ion, &c.	*Talfourd, et al.*	4453
Iowa as it is	*Parker*	580
Iron Cousin, The (2 copies) .	*Mrs. Clarke*	4850–1
Irvingiana	*Duyckinck, et al.*	923
Isaac T. Hopper : A True Life .	*Mrs. Child*	1398
Isabella Orsini	*Guerrazzi*	5059
Islamism	*Neale*	619–20
Island of Cuba	*Humboldt*	1900
" World of the Pacific . .	*Cheever*	1929
Israel Potter	*Melville*	5261
Italian Legends	*Cummings*	4840

Title	Author	No.
Italy	*Abbott*	529
"	*Spalding*	697–9
" and the Italians . . .	*von Raumer*	1725–6
" in Transition	*Arthur*	1727
" Spain and Portugal . . .	*Beckford*	1730
It is Never too Late to Mend (2 copies)	*Reade*	5399–5402
Ivanhoe	*Scott*	5479
Ixion in Heaven, &c.	*D'Israeli*	4938
Jack Hinton	*Lever*	5872
Jack in the Forecastle	*Sleeper*	5549
Tack Tier (2 copies)	*Cooper*	4781–2
Jacob Faithful	*Marryat*	4619
Jacqueline of Holland	*Grattan*	5061
" Pascal	*Cousin, et al.*	2818
Jane Eyre (2 copies)	*Miss Bronte*	4712–13
Jane Talbot	*Brown*	4707
Japan	*Hildreth*	629
Jeames' Diary, and Fitz Boodle .	*Thackeray*	5624
Jerusalem Delivered	*Tasso*	4328
John Halifax	*Miss Muloch*	5272
Johnsoniana	*Croker*	1122
Joseph Andrews, &c.	*Fielding*	5021
Journal of a Tour	*Parker*	1854
" " Voyage to Africa . .	*Carnes*	1805
" of an African Cruiser, edited by	*Hawthorne*	1820
" " Exp. to the Niger .	*Bros. Lander*	1953–4
" of Conversations with Byron	*Lady Blessington*	1128
" " " Napoleon	*Las Cases*	1222–5
" Music, vols. v.-xiv. . .	*Dwight*	7997–8001
" Researches Round the World	*Darwin*	1934–5
" of the Assembly of Wisconsin, 1848–53		8769–72
" " " " 1855–6		8774–5
" " " " 1857 Ap. vol. i.		8777
" " " " 1858–60		8778–81
" " Council " 1836–48		8738–41
" " House of Rep. " 1837–47		8742–5
" " Senate " 1848–53		8746–9
" " " " 1855–6		8751–2

Title	Author	No.
Journal of the Senate of Wisconsin, 1857 Ap. vol. i.		8754
" " " " 1858–60		8755–8
" " Texian Expedition .	*Green*	1523
" " U. S. H. of Rep., 1855-60	*Forney, et al.*	8372–8
" " " Senate, 1855–60	*Dickins, et al.*	8211–15
" " Wis. Constitutional Conven., 1846–7		8801–2
" of Voyages and Travels	*Tyreman and Bennet*	1919–21
Journey Due North . . .	*Sala*	1744
" in the Back Country .	*Olmsted*	1875
" " Seaboard Slave States .	"	1877
" throughout Ireland .	*Inglis*	1680
" through Texas . .	*Olmsted*	1873
" " the Chinese Empire	*Huc*	1787–8
" to Ararat . .	*Parrott*	1767
" Central Africa .	*Taylor*	1808
" Iceland	*M'me Pfeiffer*	1931
Julian	*Ware*	4491
Junius' Letters, edited by *Wade*		2248–9
Justice in the By-Ways	*Adams*	4631
Kansas and Nebraska	*Hale*	579
Kaloolah	*Mayo*	3249
Katharine Walton	*Simms*	5523
Kavanagh	*Longfellow*	5220
Kedge-Anchor	*Brady*	2529
Kelleys and the O'Kelleys, The . .	*Trollope*	5641
Kenilworth (2 copies)	*Scott*	5480–1
King of the Mountains, The	*About*	4629
King's Own	*Marryat*	4620
Knickerbocker Magazine, The, vols. xxxiv.-lvii., edited by *W. G. and L. G. Clark* . .		7261–84
Knick-Knacks	*Clark*	3235
Knight of Gwynne	*Lever*	5873–4
Knitting Work wrought by Mrs. Partington	*Shillaber*	3650
Knowledge is Power	*Knight*	2231
K. N. Pepper Papers	*Morris*	3649
Koran, The, edited by *Sale*		2683
Kossuth and his Generals	*De Puy*	1284
Lacon	*Colton*	3034
Ladies of the Covenant	*Anderson*	984

Title	Author	No.
Lady-Bird	*Lady Fullerton*	5028
Lady Felicia	*Cockton*	4834
Lady Lee's Widowhood	*Hamley*	5840
Lady's 2nd Voyage	*M'me Pfeiffer*	1933
" " Round the World, A	" "	1932
Lake Ngami	*Andersson*	1512
" Regions of Central Africa	*Burton*	1514
" Superior	*Agassiz*	1591
Lalla Rookh	*Moore*	4260
Lamp Lighter	*Miss Cummins*	4841
Land, Labor and Gold	*Howitt*	1800–1
Land Office Report, 1848—Appendix		7593
Lands of the Saracen	*Taylor*	1769
Lanmere	*Mrs. Dorr*	4900
La Plata, &c.	*Page*	1531
Last Days Pompeii	*Bulwer*	4667
" of the Barons	"	4668
" of the Mohicans (3 copies)	*Cooper*	4783–5
" Seven Years of H. Clay	*Colton*	918
Laurie Todd	*Galt*	5048
Lavinia	*Ruffini*	5370
Law Dictionary, A	*Burrell*	7900–1
" Lexicon	*Wharton*	7902
Laws of Business	*Parsons*	2174
" Michigan, 1833		8849
Lays of Ancient Rome, &c.	*Macaulay*	4258
" the Scottish Cavaliers	*Aytoun*	4083
Leaves from an Actor's Note-Book	*Vandenhoff*	3251
Lectures and Essays, vol. ii.	*Giles*	3341
" and Life of *Lola Montez*		1237
" on Agricultural Chemistry	*Johnston*	2508
" American Literature	*Knapp*	3506
" on Ancient History	*Niebuhr*	9–11
" on Architecture and Painting	*Ruskin*	3604
" on Art	*Allston*	3594
" on Dramatic Literature	*Hazlitt*	3157
" on Ethnography, &c.	*Niebuhr*	7–8
" on General Literature	*Montgomery*	3716
" on Logic	*Hamilton*	2970

Title	Author	No.
Life of Schamyl	*Mackie*	1296
" Schiller, F.	*Carlyle*	1275
" Scott, T.	*Scott*	841
" " W.	*Headley*	1323
" " "	*Mansfield*	1335
" Smith, J.	*Simms*	1118
" Sterling, J.	*Carlyle*	1134
" Steuben, F. W. von	*Kapp*	1316
" Talleyrand, Prince . . .	*McHarg*	1244
" Tecumseh	*Drake*	1362
" *Trenck, Baron, F.*		1469
" Washington	*Everett*	1315
" "	*Irving*	888–92
" "	*Marshall*	893–4
" "	*Paulding*	1473–4
" "	*Sparks*	896
" Watt, J.	*Muirhead*	1145
" Wellington, Duke of . .	*Bonar*	1452
" " " . .	*Stocqueler*	818
" Wesley, J.	*Southey*	1404
" William the Conquerer . . .	*Roscoe*	1097
" Wolsey, T.	*Galt*	1389
" Wright, S.	*Jenkins*	1336
" Struggle, A	*Miss Pardoe*	5343
" Thoughts	*Beecher*	3312
" Travels and Books of Humboldt .	*Taylor*	1282
" Without and Life Within	*Countess D' Ossoli*	3311
Lights and Shadows of English Life .	*Mrs. Leslie*	5234
" " Scottish Life	*Wilson*	5688
Lily and Totem	*Simms*	5524
Linwoods, The	*Miss Sedgwick*	5545–6
Lionel Lincoln	*Cooper*	4786
List of Private Claims before the U. S. Senate, '56-7		8321
Literary and Historical Miscellanies	*Bancroft*	3537
" History of the Middle Ages	*Berington*	3325
" Life of Lady Blessington .	*Madden*	1160–1
" Recreations	*Whittier*	3349
" Reminiscences . . .	*De Quincey*	3116–17
" Sketches and Letters of Lamb	*Talfourd*	1125

Title	Author	No.
Little Dorrit	*Dickens*	4916–17
Little Ellie	*Andersen*	4612
Lives	*Plutarch*	760
Lives and Letters of Abelard and Heloise	*Wight*	1074
" Voyages of Early Navigators		1412
" Works of Angelo and Raphael	*Duppa & De Quincy*	1300
Lives of American Merchants, vol. i. .	*Hunt*	801
" Ancient Philosophers . .	*Fenelon*	1418
" Atrocious Judges . . .	*Hildreth*	982
" British Dramatists .	*Campbell, et al.*	981
" " Lawyers . . .	*Roscoe*	951–2
" " Statesmen .	*Mackintosh, et al.*	969–75
" Calebrated Travellers . .	*St. John*	1415–17
" Italian Poets . . .	*Stebbing*	1080-2
" Jay and Hamilton . .	*Renwick*	1427
" Men of Letters . . .	*Brougham*	948
" Painters, &c. . . .	*Vasari*	1075–9
" Painters and Sculptors .	*Cunningham*	1422–6
Lives of the Chief Justices . .	*Campbell*	775–7
" " " . . .	*Flanders*	795–6
" Lord Chancellors . .	*Campbell*	768–74
" Poets	*Cary*	954
" "	*Johnson*	953
" Queens of England .	*Miss Strickland*	778–83
" " " before the Conquest	*Mrs. Hall*	784
" " Scotland	*Miss Strickland*	961–8
" Signers	*Dwight*	1038
Living Age, vols. i.–ix., edited by *Littell* . .		6959–67
" " " xx.–xxxi " . .		6979–90
" " " xl.–lxx. " . .		6999–7029
Locke Amsden	*Thompson*	5649
Logic in Theology, &c. . . .	*Taylor*	3335
" of Politicol Economy, &c. .	*De Quincey*	3326
Loiterings in Europe	*Corson*	1625
London Labor and London Poor, vols. i.–iii.	*Mayhew*	2200–2
" Quarterly Review, The (odd nos.) . .		7043–4
" " " vols. lxxxii.–ix. .		7046–9
" " " xci.–cix. . . .		7051–9
Lord Montagu's Page	*James*	5160

Marble Faun (2 copies) . . . . *Hawthorne* 5084–7
Marchioness of Brinvilliers . . . . *Smith* 5569
Mardi . . . . *Melville* 5262–3
Margaret Percival . . . . *Miss Sewell* 5558–9
Mark Wilton . . . . *Tayler* 5650
Martin Chuzzlewit (2 copies) . . *Dickens* 4918, 5823
Martins of Cro' Martin . . . . . *Lever* 5876
Martyrs, The . . . . . *Chateaubriand* 4828
" of Science . . . . . *Brewster* 1430
Masterman Ready . . . . . *Marryat* 4545
Mathematical Dictionary . . *Davis and Peck* 7924
Matthew Caraby . . . . . *Brothers Abbott* 3204
Maurice Tiernay . . . . . . *Lever* 5841
Meaning of Words . . . . . *Johnson* 3751
Medals of the Creation . . . . *Mantell* 2377–8
Meditations and Contemplations . . *Hervey* 2862
Meister Karl's Sketch-Book . . . . *Leland* 3218
Mellichampe (2 copies) . . . . *Simms* 5525–7
Memoir of Aikin, J. . . . . *Lucy Aikin* 842
" *Channing, W. E.* 1391–3
" Hale, D. . . . . *Thompson* 919
" Judson, A. . . . . *Wayland* 1395–6
" More, Hannah . . . . *Roberts* 1162–3
" Orleans, Duchess of . . *Schubert* 1242
" Parsons, T. . . . . . *Parsons* 1340
" Peter the Great . . . *Barrow* 1468
" *Prentiss, S. S.* 1346–7
" Ware, H., Jr. . . . . . *Ware* 1350
" Ware, Mrs. M. L. . . . *Hall* 1361
Memoirs and Correspondence of T. Moore *Russell* 851–2
" Sermons of G. Whitefield . *Gillies* 850
" of Abernethy, J. . . . . *Macilwain* 1133
" an American Lady . . *Mrs. Grant* 1359
" *Bonaparte, L.* 1231
" Buckminster, J. and J. S. *Eliza B. Lee* 1352
" Burke, E. . . . . . *Prior* 821
" *Catharine, II.* 1295
" Celebrated Characters . *Lamartine* 998–1000
" *Cellini, B.* 1312

Mimic Life	*Mrs. Ritchie*	5380
Minister's Wooing (2 copies) .	*Mrs. Stowe*	5510–11
Minstrelsy, Ancient and Modern, edited by	*Motherwell*	4268–9
Mirabeau: A Life History . . .	*Smith*	1243
Miscellanea	*Spalding*	3541
Miscellaneous Doc. of U. S. Congress (pamphlets)		8672–5
" " " House of Rep., 1855-60		8501–15
" " " Senate, 1855-60		8279–86
Miscellaneous Essays . . .	*Alison*	3550
" " . . .	*De Quincey*	3346
" Pamphlets		8883–5
" Periodicals		7334–6
" Theological Works, .	*Swedenborg*	2755
" Works of *Arnold, T.* . . .		3540
" " *Mackenzie, H.* . .		3320
" " *Sidney, Sir P.* . .		4046
" Writings of *Story J.* . . .		3539
Miscellanies	*Chalmers*	2719
"	*Emerson*	3328
Miss Gilbert's Career (2 copies) . .	*Holland*	5104–5
" Slimmens' Window . .	*Mrs. Peabody*	3215
Mission and Travels in Africa . .	*Livingstone*	1515
Mr. Brown's Letters . . .	*Thackeray*	3207
" " and Punch's Novelists	"	5627
Mr. Midshipman Easy . . .	*Marryat*	4621
Mrs. Caudle's Lectures . . .	*Jerrold*	3639
Moby Dick	*Melville*	5264
Modern British Plutarch	*Taylor*	956
" Domestic Medicine , . .	*Thomas*	2592
" French Literature . .	*Vericour*	3323
" History	*Michelet*	659
" Painters	*Ruskin*	2599–3603
" Pilgrims	*Wood*	4478–9
" Poets of Spain, translated and edited by	*Kennedy*	4044
Monaldi	*Allston*	4640
Monarchs retired from Business . .	*Doran*	3139–40
Monastery, The (2 copies)	*Scott*	5482–3
Money, &c.	*Bulwer, et al.*	4454
Money-King, &c.	*Saxe*	4333

Title	Author	No.
Monikins, The	Cooper	4791
Month in England, A.	Tuckerman	1658
Monthly Journal of Agriculture	Skinner	2477–8
Monuments of Egypt	Hawks	386
Moral History of Women	Legouve	3699
Moral Reflections, &c.	Rochefoucault	3035
Morals, by Way of Abstract	Seneca	3079
Mormons, The	Gunnison	3045
" at Home	Mrs. Ferris	3045
Mosses from an Old Manse	Hawthorne	3255
Mother's Recompense	Grace Aguilar	4638
Mt. Vernon Papers	Everett	3169
Mud Cabin, The	Isham	1657
Municipal History of Boston	Quincy	354
My Diary in India	Russell	1779–80
" Imprisonments	Pellico	1297
" Schools and Schoolmasters	Miller	1146
" Uncle Hobson and I	Jones	5173
Mysteries of Paris	Sue	5900
" Udolpho, The	Mrs. Radcliffe	5379
Na Motu	Perkins	1603
Naomi	Mrs. Webb	4482
Napoleon and his Marshals	Headley	1015–16
" Dynasty	Williams	766
Napoleonic Ideas	L. Napoleon	2253
Napoleon III. in Italy	Mrs. Browning	4106
Narrative of a Journey through India	Heber	1777–8
" Residence in Siam	Neale	1789
" Second Voyage	Ross	1502
" Visit to the Syrian Church	Southgate	1766
" Voyage to the N. W. Coast	Franchere	1852
" an Expedition to the Polar Sea	Wrangell	1957
" Criminal Trials	Feuerbach	2270
" Discovery in Africa	Jameson, et al.	1955
" " in the Polar Seas	Leslie, et al.	1956
" the Arctic Expedition	Back	1503
" the Dead Sea Expedition	Lynch	1497
" the Expl. Expedition in '42	Fremont	1857
" the Mission to Bokhara	Wolff	1498

Title	Author	No.
Narrative of the Mission to China and Japan	*Oliphant*	1493
" the Red River Expedition	*Hind*	1505–6
" the Santa Fe Expedition	*Kendall*	1869–70
" the Search for Sir J. Franklin	*M' Clintock*	1940
" the U. S. Expl. Expedition	*Wilkes*	1486–90
" " Japan Expedition	*Hawks*	1472
" " " " (Gov. Ed.)	*Hawks, et al.*	7420–22
" an Old Traveller	*Knelb*	1936
Natural History of Birds	*Rennie*	2453
" " of Enthusiasm	*Taylor*	3038
" " of Insects	*Rennie*	2451–2
" " of Man	*Prichard*	2317–18
" " of Quadrupeds	*Rennie*	2459
" " of Selborne	*White*	2368
" " of the Elephant	*Rennie*	2454
Naturalist's Library	*Gould*	2315
Natural Theology	*Paley*	2848
" " (H. F. L.)	"	2944–5
Nature and Human Nature	*Haliburton*	3242
" the Supernatural	*Bushnell*	2698
Naval History of the U. S.	*Cooper*	345
Ned Myers (2 copies)	"	4792–3
Nemesis (2 copies)	*Marion Harland*	5116–17
Neighbors, the (2 copies)	*Miss Bremer*	4693–5
Nestorians, The	*Grant*	2791
New Am. Cyclopædia, vols. i.-xi., ed. by	*Ripley & Dana*	7791–7801
New and Copious Latin Lexicon	*Leverett*	7892
" the Old, The	*Palmer*	1851
New Church Essays	*Wilkinson, et al.*	3548
" Classical Dictionary, A, edited by	*Anthon*	7898
Newcomes, The	*Thackeray*	5845
New England History	*Elliott*	277–8
" Theocracy, The	*Uhden*	2792
" Gazetteer of the U. S.	*Darby and Dwight*	7908
" History of the Conquest of Mexico, A	*Wilson*	321
" New Home—Who'll Follow?	*Mrs. Kirkland*	1844
" Priest in Conception Bay, The	*Lowell*	5200–1
" Stories	*Dickens*	4919
" Universal Gazetteer	*Williams*	7930

Title	Author	No.
New York Documents, &c., (pamphlets) . .		8844–6
Nicaraugua : Its People, &c. . .	*Squier*	1524–5
Nicholas Nickleby (2 copies) . .	*Dickens*	4920, 5822
Night and Morning	*Bulwer*	4671
Nile Notes	*Curtis*	1818
Ninety Days' Worth of Europe . . .	*Hale*	1643
'98 and '48	*Savage*	502
Nineveh and its Remains . . .	*Layard*	1494–5
Noctes Ambrosianæ	*Wilson*	3378–81
North American Review, vols. lxvi.-lxxiii.		5997-6004
" " " " lxxv.-xcii.		6006–23
" British Review, The, vols. xii.-xxix		7083–91
Northern Antiquities	*Mallet*	525
" Travel	*Taylor*	1748
Notes from Plymouth Pulpit . .	*Beecher*	2897
" of a Journey to Grand Cairo .	*Thackeray*	1813
" " Military Reconnoisance . .	*Emory*	1522
" of Travel in Italy	*Norton*	1731
" on Central America . . .	*Squier*	1596
" on Duelling	*Sabine*	3322
" on Nursing . .	*Miss Nightingale*	2606
" on the North West . .	*Bradford*	578
" " " " . . .	*Burnet*	314
Nothing to Wear	*Butler*	4110
Novels and Miscellaneous Works of *De Foe*		3415–17
Now and Then	*Warren*	5693
Nubia and Abyssinia . , . . .	*Russell*	741
Oak Openings (3 copies) . .	*Cooper*	4794–6
Obituary Add's on the death of W. R. King,	*Everett, et al*	924
Obscure Diseases of the Brain . .	*Winslow*	2591
Observations in Europe . . .	*Durbin*	1619–20
" the East . .	"	1760–1
" on Popular Antiquities	*Brand*	462–4
Occasional Productions . .	*Rush*	3542
Occult Sciences . .	*Smedley, et al.*	3063
Ocean, The	*Gosse*	2311
Odd Leaves from the Note Book of a Swamp Doctor	*Tensas*	3234
Odd People (2 copies)	*Reid*	2369–70
Odoherty Papers, ...	*Maginn*	3355–6

Title	Author	No.
Overland Journey	*Simpson*	1605
" " to San Francisco	*Greeley*	1865
Over the Cliffs	*Charlotte Chanter*	4829
Pacific and Indian Oceans	*Reynolds*	1491
Painting : Its Rise and Progress		3592
Palestine	*Osborn*	383
"	*Russell*	732
Pampinea, &c.	*Aldrich*	4089
Panorama, The, &c.	*Whittier*	4352
Papers for the Teacher	*Barnard*	3786–7
Paris Sketch-Book	*Thackeray*	1687
Partisan, The (2 copies)	*Simms*	5528–30
Pasha Papers, The	*Howe*	3202
Passages from my Autobiography	*Lady Morgan*	1166
" from the Diary of a Late Physician	*Warren*	4606–8
Pastor's Fire-Side, The	*Miss Porter*	5353–4
Past, Present and Future	*Cary*	2196
Pathfinder, The (3 copies)	*Cooper*	4797–9
Paul and Virginia	*St. Pierre*	5573
Paul Clifford	*Bulwer*	4672
Paul Fane	*Willis*	5689
Paul Ferroll	*Lady Clive*	5736
Peasant Life in Germany	*Miss Johnson*	1698
Peg Wolffington (2 copies)	*Reade*	5405–6
Pelham	*Bulwer*	4673
Pencillings by the Way	*Willis*	1652
Penny Cyclopædia, vols. ii.–vi.		7857–61
People I Have Met	*Willis*	3131
Pericles and Aspasia	*Landor*	3569–70
Perilous Adventure	*Davenport*	1950
Permanent Way, &c., of European Railways	*Colburn and Holley*	7693
Personal History of L'd Bacon	*Dixon*	1119
" Memoirs of *J. T. Buckingham*		1353–4
" Narrative of a Pilgrimage	*Burton*	1776
" " Expl. and Incidents	*Bartlett*	1518–19
" " Travels in America	*Humboldt*	1897–9
" Recollections of the Stage	*Wood*	1312
Pioneers, The (2 copies)	*Cooper*	4802–3

Personal Sketches of his own Times *Barrington* 1184
Peter Schlemihl in America . . . *Wood* 1840
Petty Annoyances of Married Life . . *Balzac* 4725
Peveril of the Peak (2 copies) . . *Scott* 5486–7
Philip Van Artevelde . . . . *Taylor* 4461
Philosophers and Actresses . . . *Houssaye* 1003–4
Philosophical Dictionary . . . *Voltaire* 7903
Philosophy in Sport . . . . *Paris* 2396
" of *Sir W. Hamilton* 2967
" History . . . . *Schlegel* 436
" Life . . . . " 3025
" Living . . . . *Ticknor* 3084
" Mysterious Agents . . *Rogers* 3047
" of the Moral Feelings . *Abercrombie* 3082
" " Sciences (abridged) . *Comte* 2242
" " Voice . . . . *Rush* 2973
Philothea . . . . . . *Mrs. Child* 4830
Phrenology . . . . . . *Spurzheim* 2594–5
Physical Atlas of Natural Phenomena *Johnston* 7941
" Geography . . *Mary Somerville* 2382
" " of the Sea . . . *Maury* 2291
Physiology of Common Life . . *Lewes* 2359–60
Piazzi Tales . . . . . . *Melville* 5265
Picciola . . . . *Saintine* 5554
Pickwick Papers (2 copies) . . . *Dickens* 4928, 5827
Pic-Nic Papers . . . . *Dickens, et al.* 1595
Pictorial Field-Book . . . . *Lossing* 339–40
" History of New York . . *Barber* 290
Picture-Book without Pictures . *Andersen* 4613
Pictures from St. Petersburg . . *Jerrnann* 1746
" of Country Life . . . *Miss Carey* 4845
" " Travel in France . . *Dumas* 1684
Pilgrimage to Egypt . . . . *Smith* 1812
" to the Holy Land . . . *Lamartine* 1762–3
Pilgrims of the Rhine . . . *Bulwer* 4674
Pilgrim's Progress, The . . . . *Bunyan* 2701
Pillar of Fire . . . . . . *Ingraham* 4475
Pilot, The (2 copies) . . . . . *Cooper* 4800–1
Piney Woods Tavern, or Sam Slick in Texas . . 3239

Title	Author	No.
Pioneers, Preachers, &c.	*Milburn*	2821
Pirate, The (2 copies)	*Scott*	5484–5
Plain Talk about Fruits, &c.	*Beecher*	2511
Planetary and Stellar Worlds	*Mitchel*	2409
Plant Hunters (2 copies)	*Reid*	4553, 7
Plays	*Mrs. Ritchie*	4451
" and Poems	*Boker*	4445–6
" of *P. Massinger*		4404
Plea for Amusements	*Sawyer*	3836
Pleasant Memories	*Sigourney*	1648
Pluribustah	*Thomson*	3633
Poems	*Arnold*	4086
"	*Brainard*	4115
"	*Browning*	4102–3
"	*Mrs. Browning*	4104–5
"	*Bryant*	4099
"	*Mrs. Butler*	4108
"	*De Vere*	4157
"	*Emerson*	4168
"	*Holmes*	4198
"	*Hood*	4200–3
"	*Lindsay*	4239
"	*Longfellow*	4242–3
"	*Lowell*	4236–7
"	*Massey*	4385
"	*Parsons*	4288
"	*Saxe*	4334
"	*Smith*	4320
"	*Tennyson*	4324–5
"	*Willis*	4349
" and Ballads	*Goethe*	4183
" of Ossian, "translated" by *Macpherson*		4280
" of *Shakspeare*		4335
Poetical and Prose Writings of *Sprague, C.*		4332
" Works of *Akenside, M.*		4080
" " *Beattie, J.*		4114
" " *Butler, S.*		4112–13
" " *Byron, Lord*		4040
" " *Chatterton, T.*		4127–8

Title	Author	No.
Preacher and the King, The	*Bungener*	2819
Pre-Adamite Earth	*Harris*	2849
Precaution (2 copies)	*Cooper*	4805–6
Prenticeana	*Prentice*	3646
Pre-Raphaelitism	*Ruskin*	3506
President's Daughters, The	*Miss Bremer*	4696
Price of a Crown	*Sue*	5563
Pride and Prejudice, &c	*Miss Austen*	4624
Priest and the Huguenot, The	*Bungener*	4483–4
Prince of the House of David	*Ingraham*	4476
Principles of Chemistry	*Stockhardt*	2403
" Eloquence	*Maury*	3081
" Physics	*Muller*	2301
" Physiology	*Combe*	2465
" Psychology	*Spencer*	2962
" Science	*Potter*	2535
" Social Science	*Carey*	2044–6
" Zoology	*Agassiz and Gould*	2361
Private Correspondence of *Cowper*		839
" " *Webster*		916–17
" Journal of *A. Burr*		911–12
Probabilities	*Tupper*	2869
Probable Fall in the Value of Gold	*Chevalier*	2198
Professor, The	*Miss Bronte*	4714
" at the Breakfast-Table	*Holmes*	3232
Progress of Religious Ideas	*Mrs. Child*	2807–9
Pronouncing Spanish Dictionary	*Velasquez*	7893
Prose and Poetry of Europe and America—edited by *Morris and Willis*		3498
" Works of *Milton*		2695–6
" Writers of America, edited by *Griswold*		3500
" " Germany, " *Hedge*		3499
Proverbial Philosophy	*Tupper*	4323
Provincial Letters	*Pascal*	2860
Prue and I	*Curtis*	3237
Public and Domestic Life of Burke	*Burke*	1187
" Private History of Napoleon III.	*Smucker*	1232
" " Life of Eldon, L'd	*Twiss*	822–3
" " " Webster,	*Lyman*	1332

Title	Author	No.
Public Life of J. Brown,	*Redpath*	1342
" Men of the Revolution	*Sullivan*	800
Pulpit of the Revolution	*Thornton*	2901
Punch (London) vols. xxxvi.-xl.		7748–51
Punch's Letters	*Jerrold*	3641
Puritans, The	*Hopkins*	2660–1
Pursuit of Knowledge under Difficulties	*Craik*	1435–6
Putnam's Magazine, vols. i.-x.		5967–76
Quadroon, The	*Reid*	5388
Quakerism	*Mrs. Greer*	3042
Q. Review, The, vol. ii. (third N. Y. series) ed. by	*Brownson*	7339
Queechy	*Miss Warner*	5676–7
Queen of Hearts	*Collins*	4849
Queens and Princesses of France	*White*	1437
" of Society	*Grace and Philip Wharton*	3132
Quentin Durward (2 copies)	*Scott*	5488–9
Quits	*Baroness Tautphœus*	5635
Quodlibet	*Kennedy*	3209
Races of Man	*Pickering*	2354
Rachel and the New World	*Beauvallet*	1841
Rag-Bag, The	*Willis*	3220
Rail Road Reports (pamphlets)		8881
Rambler, The, Idler, The, &c.	*Johnson, et al.*	3554
" in Mexico,	*Latrobe*	1867
Rambles among Words	*Swinton*	3757
" in Sweden, &c.		1568
Ran Away to Sea	*Reid*	4554
Rational Defence of the Gospel	*Watts*	2867
Reason and Faith	*Rogers*	2845
Rebellion Record, The, edited by *Moore*		334
Recent Enquiries in Theology ("Essays and Reviews")—	*Temple, et al.*	2851
" Progress in Astronomy	*Loomis*	2407
" Speeches and Addresses	*Sumner*	3935
Recollections of a Journey through Tartary, &c.	*Huc*	1793–4
" " Life-time	*Goodrich*	1344–5
" " Literary Life	*Miss Mitford*	1164
" " Policeman	*Waters*	3238
" of Egypt	*Baroness von Minutoli*	1809

Title	Author	No.
Ruth	*Mrs. Gaskell*	5054
Rutledge (2 copies)	*Miss Dowe (?)*	4832–3
Sable Cloud, The	*Adams*	4639
Sacred History of the World	*Turner*	2940–2
Sacred Poems	*Vaughan*	4343
St. Giles and St. James	*Jerrold*	5172
St. Ronan's Well (2 copies)	*Scott*	5492–3
Saint Leger	*Kimball*	3248
St. Leon	*Godwin*	5064
St. Valentine's Day (2 copies)	*Scott*	5494–5
Salad for the Social	*Saunders*	3195
" " Solitary	"	3194
Salathiel	*Croly*	4837–8
Salmagundi	*Irving and Paulding*	3200
Salt Water Bubbles	*Sleeper*	5548
Sand-Hills of Jutland	*Andersen*	4630
Sartor Resartus, &c.	*Carlyle*	3124
Satanstoe (2 copies)	*Cooper*	4810–11
Satires of *Juvenal, et al.*		4223
Say and Seal (2 copies)	*Misses Warner*	5678–81
Sayings and Doings of Sam Slick	*Haliburton*	3240
Scalp Hunters, The	*Reid*	5390
Scampavias	*Wise*	1757
Scandinavia	*Crichton and Wheaton*	709–10
Scarlet Letter, The	*Hawthorne*	5088
Scenes and Legends	*Miller*	5300
" in Practice	*Dixon*	4906
" in Spain	*Poco Mas*	1715
School Architecture	*Barnard*	2532
" Days at Rugby	*Hughes*	5078
Scientific American, vols. viii.-xiv		7977–83
" " " i.-iv. N. S.		7984–7
" Phenomena	*Gower*	2355
Scotland and the Scotch	*Miss Sinclair*	1679
Scottish Chiefs, The	*Miss Porter*	5355–6
Scouring the White Horse	*Hughes*	5074
Scout, The	*Simms*	5533
Sea, The (La Mer)	*Michelet*	3900

Title	Author	No.
Sea Lions, The (2 copies) . . .	*Cooper*	4812–13
Second Visit to the U. S. . . .	*Lyell*	1833–4
Sec. of the Treas. Acc. of Receipts and Expenditures, 1855-60,	*Guthrie, et al.*	8639–43
Secret History of the French Court .	*Cousin*	1235
" Passion, The . . .	*Williams*	5903
Select British Eloquence . . .	*Goodrich*	3913
Select British Poets—Falconer to Scott, ed. by	*Frost*	4042
" " " Southey to Croly	"	4043
" Minor Poems . .	*Goethe and Schiller*	4180
" Poetical Works of *J. Montgomery* . .		4257
" Speeches	*Canning*	3917
" Works of *T. Smollett*		5897
Selection of Legal Maxims . . .	*Broom*	2172
Selections from the American Poets, ed. by	*Bryant*	4381
" " British Classics	*Blair, et al.*	4116
" " " Poets, edited by	*Halleck*	4383–4
" " Works of *Sir T. More* . .		3710
" " Writings of *W. S. Landor* .		3330
Self-Control	*Miss Brunton*	4720
Self-Help	*Smiles*	1037
Self-Made Men	*Seymour*	1036
Semi-Detached House . .	*Lady Lewis*	5226
Sense and Sensibility, &c . .	*Miss Austin*	4625
Sermons	*Chalmers*	2721–2
"	*Kingsley*	2902
"	*Spurgeon*	2890–5
"	*Trench*	2896
" for the People . .	*Huntington*	2912
" Lectures, &c., delivered in Ireland	*Wiseman*	1681
" of Theism, &c. . . .	*Parker*	2911
Session Laws of Wis., 1837-58		8787–95
Seven Lamps of Architecture . .	*Ruskin*	3605
Seven Years in Central America . .	*Froebel*	1597
Seventh Census of the U. S., 1850 .	*DeBow*	7403
Shakspeare and his Friends . .	*Williams*	5901
" Papers	*Maginn*	3172
Shakspeare's Legal Acquirements .	*Campbell*	3148
" Scholar	*White*	3536

Title	Author	No.
Twenty Years After	*Dumas*	4905
" " of an African Slaver	*Canot*	1806
Twice Married	*Philleo*	5739
" Told Tales	*Hawthorne*	5089–90
Twin Roses	*Mrs. Ritchie*	5381
Twins, The	*Tupper*	5652
Two Admirals, The (2 copies)	*Cooper*	4816–17
Two Hundred Lyrical Poems	*Beranger*	4100
Two Lives	*Miss McIntosh*	5286
Two Millions	*Butler*	4109
Two Paths, The	*Ruskin*	3607
Two Years Ago	*Kingsley*	5183
Two Years before the Mast	*Dana*	1939
Tylney Hall	*Hood*	5071
Typee	*Melville*	1923
Types of Mankind	*Nott and Gliddon*	2316
Ugly Duck, The	*Andersen*	4615
Uncle Tom's Cabin	*Mrs. Stowe*	5512–13
Undine, and Sintram	*Fouque*	5029
United States Exploring Expeditions	*Jenkins*	1485
" " Grinnell Expedition	*Kane*	1499
U. S. Mag. and Dem. Review, vols. xxii.–xxxi., edited by *Kettell, et al.*		5987–96
" Naval Astronomical Exp'ns, vols. i.-iii.	*Gilliss*	7405–7
" " " " vol. vi.	"	7410
Universal History	*Tytler and Nares*	642–7
" Gazetteer	*M'Culloch*	7906–7
Useful Arts	*Bigelow*	2536–7
Use of the Body	*Moore*	3031
Up the Rhine	*Hood*	3635–6
Vagabond Life in Mexico	*Ferry*	1868
Valentine Vox (2 copies)	*Cockton*	5816–17
Vale of Cedars, The	*Grace Aguilar*	4635
Vanity Fair (vol. iii.)		7958
" " (2 copies)	*Thackeray*	5851–2
Vasconselos	*Simms*	5535
Vathek	*Beckford*	4719
Vegetable Substances	*Lankester*	2617
Venetia	*D'Israeli*	4936

Title	Author	No.
Woman's Thoughts about Women, A	*Miss Muloch*	3696
Women Artists	*Mrs. Ellet*	3610
" of Israel, The	*Grace Aguilar*	3122–3
Woodcraft (2 copies)	*Simms*	5536–7
Woods and Waters	*Street*	3898
Woodstock (2 copies)	*Scott*	5506–7
Works of *Adams, J.*		2099–2108
" *Ames, F.*		2087–8
" *Bacon, Lord*		2956–8
" *Beaumont, and Fletcher*		4405–15
" *Bolinbroke, Lord*		2983–6
" *Browne, Sir T.*		2979–82
" *Burke, E.*		2015–17
" *Burns, R.*		4053
" *Calhoun, J. C.*		2125–8
" *Channing, W. E.*		2811–16
" *Chesterfield, Lord*		3584
" *Cowper, W.*		4052
" *Dick, T.*		2700
" *Dryden, J.*		4048–9
" *Franklin, B.*		2089–98
" *Goldsmith, O.*		3392–5
" *Hooker, R.*		2693–4
" *Horace*		4197
" *Johnson, S.*		3512–13
" *Jonson, B.*		4418–26
" *Josephus, J.*		1–2
" *Lamb, C.*		3422–3
" *Landor, W. S.*		3514–15
" *Marlowe, C.*		4403
" *Mitford, Miss M. R.*		3520
" *Montaigne, M. de*		3015–18
" *More, Hannah*		3509–10
" *Paley, W.*		3087–91
" *Plato*		3396–3401
" *Poe, E. A.*		3418–21
" *Rabelais, F.*		3444–5
" *St. Pierre, J. H. B. de*		3446–7
" *Seward, W. H.*		2109–11

SYNOPSIS

OF THE

CLASSIFICATION ON THE SHELVES.

I. *History*—(Nos. 1 to 759.)—Ancient, Mediæval and Modern, Universal, National, Local, and of Races; Geography; Ethnography; Chronicles; Annals; Historical Diaries and Correspondence; Memoirs of Courts, Reigns and Campaigns; Philosophy of History; Manners and Customs; Antiquities, Heraldry; Episodes and Incidents.

II. *Biography*—(Nos. 760 to 1484.)—Collective and Individual; Personal Memoirs of Dynasties; Personal Diaries and Correspondence.

III. *Travels*—(Nos. 1485 to 1973.)—Universal and Local; Voyages; Scientific and Commercial Expeditions; Military Reconnoisances; Military and Nautical Adventures; Descriptions of Court and Social Life; Governmental, Religious and National Characteristics.

IV. *Political Science*—(Nos. 1974 to 2290.)—Histories of Civilization, Administrations, Conventions and Constitutions; The Collected Letters and Works of Eminent Statesmen and Diplomats; Diplomatic and Official Papers and Correspondence; Social Science; Political Economy; Congressional Debates; Jurisprudence; Statistics of Trade and Commerce; Celebrated Trials.

V. *Natural Science, Technology and Mathematics*—(Nos. 2291 to 2589.)—General and Special Treatises on the Arts and

Sciences, and the Relations between Science and Religion; Reports; Researches; Domestic Economy; Agriculture; Architecture; Surveying; Navigation; Applications of Science to Domestic and Mechanic Arts and Manufactures; Military Art and Science.

VI. *Medical Science*—(Nos. 2590 to 2637.)—Medical Jurisprudence; Popular Treatises on Medicine and Hygiene.

VII. *Theology and Philosophy*—(Nos. 2638 to 3114)—General and Local Ecclesiastical History; Histories of Denominations, Missions, The Reformation, and Religious Orders; Doctrinal Treatises; Apochryphal Books; Commentaries; Religious Philosophy; Evidences of Christianity; Entire Writings of Celebrated Divines and Philosophers; Sermons, Lectures, Discourses, Sketches and Miscellanies; Natural Theology; Practical Christianity; Psychology; Metaphysics; Ethics; Logic; Rhetoric; History of Philosophy; Free Masonry; Spiritualism; Mythology; Magic; Demonology; Superstitions; Witchcraft.

VIII. *Miscellaneous Literature*—(Nos. 3115 to 4032.)—Scientific, Historical, Biographical, Philosophical, Theological, Critical and Miscellaneous Essays; Lectures on Poetry and Dramatic Literature; Collected Works in *Belles Lettres;* Sketches of Society, Persons and Places; Desultoria; Table Talk; Facetiæ; Papers from the Periodicals; Æsthetics; Romantic Chronicles, Histories, and Travels; History of Literature; History and Philosophy of Language; Mental and Physical Recreations; Rural Occupations and Scenery; Works on Education; Didactic Letters; Orations and Speeches; Transactions of Agricultural and Historical Societies; Bibliography; Greek and Latin Text-Books; Selections in Prose and Verse; Fables.

IX. *Poetry and the Drama*—(Nos. 4033 to 4472.)—Classic and cotemporary Authors of Britain and America; Translations of Greek, Latin and Modern Continental Poets, in Prose and Verse; Songs and Ballads; Complete Works of Standard Dramatists.

X. *Fiction.*—(Nos. 4475 to 5959.)—Novels, Tales and Romances, by American, English, Scotch, Irish, German, Italian, Spanish and Oriental writers; Religious, Historical, Sentimental, Satirical, Humorous, Nautical and Professional Novels; Juvenile Stories and Adventures; Fairy Tales; Legends; Collections of Magazine Tales.

XI. *Periodicals.*—(Nos. 5960 to 6088 and 6959 to 7373.)—Literary, Critical, Scientific, Mercantile, Political, Religious, Mechanical, Musical and Miscellaneous; Reviews, Magazines, and Illustrated Papers, British and American.

XII. *Works of Reference.*—(Nos. 7774 to the end.)—Encyclopædias, General and Special; Dictionaries—English, French Spanish, Latin, Greek, Literary, Scientific, Law, Philosophical, Fine Art, Historical, Chronological, Biographical, Mythological, Genealogical, Commercial, and of Arts and Manufactures; Concordances; Publications of the Smithsonian Institution; Gazetteers, Universal and State; Atlases, General and Physical; Illustrated Works; Valuable Scientific, Agricultural, and Antiquarian Works; Journals, Reports, and Documents of Congress and the State Legislature; Commercial, Scientific and Military Expeditions authorized by Government; Astronomical, Boundary, Geological, Commercial, Financial, Land, Military, Naval, Educational, Postal, Meteorological and Sanitary Reports; Reports on Foreign Relations, The Coast Survey, Rail Road Surveys, and the Census; Presidents' and Governors' Messages and Accompanying Documents; Records of Congressional Debates *in extenso*; Reprints of Important State Papers and the Annals of Congress; Voluminous Documentary Histories; Session Laws; Revised Statutes; Codes; Reports of the State Supreme Court; Journals of Constitutional Conventions; Parliamentary Law; Records of Inventions; Bound Pamphlets,—including Speeches and Addresses, Reports of Library Associations and other Public Institutions, &c.

☞ Class XII., is composed of Works which are permanently retained in the Library for reference and consultation there only.

ERRATA.

For	Recipts,	page	10,	line	18,	read Receipts.
"	Belle,	"	44,	"	29,	" Bell.
"	Boccacio,	"	48,	"	21,	" Boccaccio.
"	Brande,	"	49,	"	4,	" Brand.
"	Adventure,	"	58,	"	19,	" Adventures.
"	Beck,	"	58,	"	20,	" Peck.
"	De Quincy,	"	59,	"	16,	" De Quincey.
"	Rudalstadt,	"	61,	"	8,	" Rudolstadt.
"	Gœthe,	"	61,	"	37,	" Goethe.
"	Report of	"	62,	"	21,	" Report on.
"	Galligher,	"	64,	"	23,	" Gallagher.
"	James, J. P. R.	"	73.	"	16,	" James, G. P. R.
"	Davenport, Dunn	"	77,	"	25,	" without a stop.
"	Macaulay,	"	79,	"	18,	" Macauley.
"	Glidden,	"	85,	"	6,	" Gliddon.
"	Phelen,	"	87,	"	29,	" Phelan.
"	Shelton,	"	96,	"	23,	" Skelton.
"	Sturn,	"	99,	"	18,	" Sturm.
"	Twedie,	"	103,	"	8,	" Tweedie.
"	Renourd,	"	104,	"	7,	" Renouard.
"	Wheeler, Miriam B.,	"	105,	"	27,	" Wicher, Mrs.
"	Stewart,	"	112,	"	14,	" Stuart.
"	Washington,	"	121,	"	10,	" the same, italicized.
"	Mrs. Bremer,	"	133,	"	25,	" Miss Bremer.
"	Tack,	"	136,	"	11,	" Jack.
"	Expedit'n,	"	139,	"	15,	" Exhibition.
"	Life in the Life,	"	141,	"	10,	" Life.
"	Adventure,	"	154,	"	30,	" Adventures.
"	Mcfarlane,	"	163,	"	20,	" Macfarlane.
"	Cooledge,	"	167,	"	26,	" Coolidge.

A few lines (Authors, under letter U,) most unaccountably got into page 89, instead of page 103.

☞ The critical reader is reminded that it was originally contemplated that some items in the Catalogue — Presidents' Messages and Periodicals, for instance — should form *continuous* entries; hence, the repetitions do not indicate the sneccessive occupants of the chair Presidential or Editorial.

www.ingramcontent.com/pod-product-compliance
Lightning Source LLC
LaVergne TN
LVHW011230110826
845150LV00006B/1596